FOCUS YOUR WRITING

FOCUS YOUR WRITING

by

BONNIE HEARN

First published in 1995 by CT Publishing, Redding, CA

Copyright © 2001 by Bonnie Hearn

All rights reserved.
No part of this book may be reproduced, stored in a retrieval system, or transmitted by any means, electronic, mechanical, photocopying, recording, or otherwise, without written permission from the author.

ISBN: 1-58820-549-5

This book is printed on acid free paper.

1stBooks – rev. 12/20/00

Bonnie Hearn

TABLE OF CONTENTS

Introduction **WHY YOU? WHY NOW?** xv
How focus can help the beginning writer publish now.

Chapter 1 **FOCUS VERSUS HOCUS POCUS** 1
Why what you may have learned about writing is myth. How to focus. Born and taught writers. Using the lonely child within. Honest writing. The basics of focus.

Chapter 2 **USING FOCUS TO SECOND-GUESS THE MARKET** 15
How magazines reveal exactly what they buy, and what the writer can learn about focus by studying titles and blurbs of published articles.

Chapter 3 **IDEAS THAT SELL (AND WHO BUYS THEM)** 23
New slants to universal themes. Trade and consumer magazines and what they buy. The Big Twelve.

Chapter 4 **FOCUS YOUR LEAD/FOCUS YOUR STORY** 39

How to create a working title that will help you focus your piece. Five leads that work and how to write them. The three P's: Promise, proof, payoff. Leads most beginners should avoid, including the dreaded Question Lead, the All-That-Glitters-Is-Not-Gold Lead and the Gimmick Lead.

Chapter 5 **THE FOCUSED WAY TO INTERVIEW JUST ABOUT ANYONE** 53

Four surprisingly easy ways to get the interview. What to ask. Changing focus. How to be the subject's new best friend. Press releases. One long quote. A short word about tape recorders.

Chapter 6 **STITCHING THE SEAMLESS ARTICLE** 65

Choosing a focus, lead and billboard statement. Selecting and varying quotes. Handling attribution, orphan quotes and multi-source articles. Connecting the facts.

Chapter 7	**THE LAST WORD, OR HOW TO FINISH WITH A BANG**	75
	How to end your article. Seven examples of endings that work and how they tie into (but don't duplicate) your lead. The relevant quote, the related fact, the last detail, the anecdote, the editorial, the joke and the imperative.	
Chapter 8	**FOCUSED EDITING: THE LAST STEP BEFORE YOU SUBMIT**	85
	Murdering adjectives, adverbs and your "darlings" before they murder your piece. Picking up the pace. How style restrictions can help you develop your own, individual style.	
Chapter 9	**THE FOCUSED WAY TO WIN**	97
	The importance of contests, and why most entries fail. How to write prize-winning poems, award-winning articles and first-class fiction. How much to pay. How to land in the handful of finalists.	

Chapter 10	**MARKETING TOOLS: QUERY, BLURB, OUTLINE, SUMMARY AND THAT DREADED SYNOPSIS**	109

The only query letter you'll ever need to write. Basics of the blurb and cover letter. The dreaded synopsis. Summary and chapter outlines. Which to use for what. Rejection fear and rejection depression. Simultaneous submissions.

Chapter 11	**YOUR TIME AS A WRITER (AND WHAT IT'S WORTH)**	131

Your four jobs as a writer. What your time is worth. How to develop your base.

Chapter 12	**CLASSES, CLUBS, CAUSES AND CONS**	141

How to evaluate the people who want to charge you for strokes. Why most writing classes won't get you published. Why the best feedback is free and where to find it.

Chapter 13	**FEAR AND VALIDATION**	153

How to use fear without being used by it. The importance of validation/publication right now.

Appendix I	**MUST-READ PUBLICATIONS**	161

| *Appendix II* | **CONTEST JUDGE'S CHEAT SHEET** | 165 |
| *Appendix III* | **MANUSCRIPT SUBMISSIONS** | 167 |

Focus Your Writing

"A professional writer is an amateur who didn't quit."

—*Richard Bach*

Focus Your Writing

Bonnie Hearn

Author's Note

I began this book after my first year of teaching writing, back when I had all the answers. Since then, I've seen many of my students go on to publish their work. I've been fortunate enough to have a comfortable free-lance career in addition to my day job as an editor. And I no longer have all the answers.

If I were to write "Focus Your Writing" today, I would make several changes. Having sold every book since this one on the basis of a proposal, I would be much more detailed in what a book proposal must contain, and I would warn writers that most book proposals are simply too much paper. A focused book proposal, I would say, can tell the story of your book in 12 pages or less.

I would also spend more time exploring the topics of fear and sabotage. Each of us has a voice on our shoulder telling us we're not good enough, telling us to wait until the kids are grown, telling us to clean the oven or wash the car before we sit down to write. As writers, we must learn how to recognize the voice and turn it down. We must also learn how to tune out others who are attempting to sabotage our writing time and our self-confidence.

Although I touch on these topics in the book, I had no idea what major pitfalls they are and how necessary it is for writers to be aware of them. Disclaimers aside, I have re-released the book because I continue to hear from writers it has helped, many who made their first sales as a result of it. I am more convinced than ever that lack of focus is what keeps many talented writers from publishing, and I believe this book will teach you how to better focus everything you write. If it helps you, or if you have questions about anything you read here, feel free to contact me at bhearn@pacbell.net.

Focus Your Writing

Much has changed in my life since I decided to teach the concept of focus almost 10 years ago, and most of it has been good change. Even after 18 years, my job as an editor has failed to diminish my passion for the written word. I concur with Flaubert that although writing may be a dog's life at times, "it is the only life worth living." If you agree, if you love writing as much as I do, you'll probably find the information you need sooner or later. My goal now, as it was in 1991, is to save you the time I wasted while trying to learn how to write and sell my work. Regardless of whether you're a beginner or a published writer, I hope that I can provide you with some of the answers you are seeking.

A writer never stops learning and growing. I still receive the greatest instruction and inspiration from my students. To edit someone's work is to know them intimately, and I have had the good fortune to edit the work of many talented people I never would have encountered any other way. I met some of my dearest friends, including my husband, in my writing class. This book is dedicated to them.

"Bonnie Hearn's book is money in the bank for freelance writers on every level. I intend to read it once a year until I'm too feeble to focus on writing or anything else." – John Clausen, Editor, *Writing for Money*.

Bonnie Hearn

To my students, who have changed my writing and my life.

Focus Your Writing

Bonnie Hearn

INTRODUCTION

WHY YOU? WHY NOW?

Chances are you've thought about being a writer most of your life. Maybe you've sold a few pieces and want to find out why you're not selling more. Perhaps you're a closet writer who's never dared admit your dream to anyone but yourself. Finally you've decided to get serious about writing for publication.

You can do it the way I did and fight your way through a sea of rejection until you learn to swim. Or you can start out knowing what I wish someone had taught me 30 years ago. In a word, focus.

Focus is what can make a talented beginner a published writer. It can get you in print at first, and it can keep you in print for the rest of your life.

I'm not suggesting it's all a writer needs. Others far more talented than I can lecture to you about unity, voice, style and countless esoteric concepts that are just as important and infinitely more difficult to master. Focus, however, is (1) relatively easy to learn and (2) the one concept that can help you publish your writing while you're still trying to figure out the finer points of craft. It's worked for me, and it's worked for enough of my students that I can't believe our successes are a series of unrelated accidents.

Focus Your Writing

Before I began teaching, I always thought my history of publication, as well as the editing job for which I am totally unqualified and ridiculously well-compensated, were the result of fool's luck and Type A drive. I had neither the audacity nor the knowledge to teach anyone how to write, and that was fine with me.

Then, in March of 1990, the writing instructor at our local adult school resigned, and someone at the school suggested me. One quick telephone interview, and I found myself hired, by default. The first night I was to meet my class, I confessed my insecurities to Linda, a trusted friend who supervises our newspaper's classified advertising department.

"How am I going to do this?" I asked her that evening before I left the office.

"You don't have to be the light, just the window that reflects it," Linda said, as if she'd been dispensing such wisdom all day.

I thought about her words as I drove to class. When I stood up to face over 20 strangers, I heard myself talking about something that was as unfamiliar to me as it appeared to be to this room of would-be writers. Focus.

I certainly didn't discover the concept. Only after I started teaching, did I realize that most of the manuscripts I rejected as an editor and as a contest judge had one flaw in common. They, like my students' work, lacked focus.

I was surprised that such an apparently simple concept can make the difference between publication and rejection. Isn't focus an automatic part of the writing process, in the same way that commas and paragraphs are? I don't think so. Something about the act of writing makes us feel we have to tell all we know about a subject. Instead of focusing on our reader, we get wrapped up in our prose, our wonderful ideas, and write what *we* need to know. This can be great fun and certainly cathartic, but it seldom results in publishable material.

In "Magazine Writing That Sells," Don McKinney, a former McCall's editor, said, "... writing is a craft. It is a profession. And it is the professionals who make money at it. Anybody can learn the techniques professionals use... Editors are looking for ideas that suit their publications, and query letters that promise solid, usable manuscripts. The writer may have sold a hundred articles or none—the *idea* is the key ingredient."

Ideas are indeed essential, but until you focus on one idea and then focus it to a specific publication, you'll be drowning in some editor's pile of slush.

As a focused writer, you must let go of *me* and think about *you*. You have to be willing to put yourself aside and focus on the needs of the readers for whom you are writing. In the chapters that follow, I'm going to show you how my students and I try to accomplish that.

My focus has been to write this with the head of an editor and the heart of a writer, understanding the needs of one and the desires of the other. From this dual perspective, I've attempted to provide you with honest, admittedly biased opinions, regarding everything from multiple submissions to writing clubs to, yes, money.

Warning. If you're like my students, you'll soon be sick of the word *focus*. Believe me, I'm sick of it, too. Yet I'm going to keep hammering, because I truly believe that learning focus is the fastest way for you to begin to reach your writing goals.

When I worked, years ago, as a radio station copywriter, I got to listen to the commercials I had written as they were aired each day through the office stereo system. At first I loved it. After a few weeks, I wanted to scream every time I heard my by-then well-memorized words. When I begged Bellman, my boss, to let me change the copy on one particularly annoying spot, he responded in the gruff, Lucky Strike voice I can still hear today. "Remember this, Hearn. By the time we get sick to death of a spot, the listener is just starting to hear it."

End of sermon. I hope that reading about and practicing focus helps you create salable manuscripts, so that, if you love writing as much as I do, you can earn satisfaction, money, (there's that word again), maybe even a living from that love affair.

Focus Your Writing

A Sufi axiom states that when the student is ready, the teacher will come. Once we're clear about an action, we're led to what we need. You're here now. Why now? Because, for whatever reason or number of reasons, you're ready.

YOUR FIRST ASSIGNMENT

Before you begin, you need to know about you. You also need to get in the habit of writing every day. Your first assignment is:

1. A one-page essay on why and what you want to write NOW. What's holding you up? What do you need to change in your life and the way you think about yourself?
2. What are your writing goals a year, five years from now?

Put your essay in a folder marked, "Focus Assignments." The answers are for you alone. They're the beginning of your search for focus.

In the next chapter, you'll learn the basis of focus and why much of what you may have heard about writing is really nothing more than a lot of hocus pocus.

Bonnie Hearn

CHAPTER ONE

FOCUS VERSUS HOCUS POCUS

The writers' magazines are filled with ads from so-called professionals promising, for a fee of course, to divulge the secrets of becoming a published writer. Maybe some of them really do know the secret. Too often, though, what these "professionals" are selling is a bunch of hocus pocus.

Perhaps studying scripts of "Murder She Wrote," memorizing the basic plots of literature, evaluating the role Greek mythology plays in romance novels or paying someone to set your lyrics to music really will get you published. There's a less esoteric (and usually less costly) route, however, one that's going to take just about everything you have to give.

Writing is what makes you a writer—working at it, focusing it, paying your dues as a person and an artist. There's nothing magical about hard work and dedication, and perhaps that's the real magic. The only way you get there, regardless of where your there happens to be, is by focusing on your goal and taking the steps that will bring you closer to it. They may be baby steps. That doesn't matter. All you want to do at this point is move.

CUTTING THROUGH THE HOCUS POCUS

Before you as much as turn on the computer, you need to free yourself of the misconceptions you may have about writing and publication. Four of the most common are:

An agent, paid for or otherwise, will get you published

Pure hocus pocus. Agent Michael Larsen puts it this way. "It's been said that an agent is like a bank loan—you can only get one if you can prove you don't need it... Nonsense! It's easy to get an agent. What's hard is writing a salable book."

While a literary agent is an invaluable tool when you're ready, no one can *get* you published until you produce a focused, marketable piece of work. That's the difficult part. It's called writing.

If you have talent, you will publish sooner or later

More hocus pocus. Some of the most talented writers on the planet fail to publish because, although they can string beautiful words together, they can't piece a story or an article together. Without focus, they ultimately choke on their own pointless prose.

The literary world consists of born writers and taught writers. You already know if you're in the former category. The knowledge was always there, born in you, even before you could put it into words. You were probably the kid who got A's in English, the adult family member praised for writing the best (and usually funniest) letters. While you're willing to do anything short of delivering newspapers to be connected with the writing world, your dream is to see your name on the cover of a novel.

The taught writer sees his craft as a not altogether pleasant means to an end. He lives with a specific story that begs to be told, often in a nonfiction format. The taught writer has something important to say but isn't certain how to say it. Both born and taught writers can benefit from focus.

To be a born writer with focus is the best of all possible worlds. Talent can't be taught. Combined with focus, which can be taught, it shines. If you're a taught writer who understands focus, you still have a better chance of publishing than the genius who can't get from Point A to Point B, let alone the rest of the story-crafting alphabet.

No one really wants to work with a beginner

True, an history of publication will attract an editor's attention, but that's all. The work must stand on its own merits, not the writer's track record.

No one starts out published. Every writer begins as a beginner. In my job as an editor, I've never hesitated to buy a focused article from a first-timer over a piece of rambling prose from a so-called pro.

When I began selling my work back in the 1970s, I was amazed that magazines that bought from me once bought twice, three times and more. Some editors even called me with ideas. A few paid expenses. All this for someone who was still a novice.

I learned the reason years later when I was offered the position as managing editor with a large publisher of pet magazines. One of my jobs would be to work with free-lancers, the editor said.

When I told her I liked working with free-lancers, she shook her head in disbelief.

"Why? Are you a masochist?"

"No, but I was a free-lancer for many years. I guess I relate to them."

"Not our free-lancers," she said. "They're sloppy. They don't respect our deadlines, and they turn into prima donnas when you try to edit them."

It was then I began to understand how important a good free-lancer is. Many will fight for the assignment. They want to be writers, but (to paraphrase Peter De Vries) what they can't stand is the paperwork.

If you've made the decision to be a free-lance writer, commit yourself to being the best you can be. Regardless of what you're writing, always try to give the editor a little more than you are being paid to produce. It will return to you many times in higher fees and repeated assignments.

It takes years to get published

This is the ultimate hocus pocus. You don't have to be a Pulitzer winner to publish. What you need is one measly piece that meets the needs of just one measly editor.

I started publishing before I was a competent writer. I was a careful writer. I was certainly a driven one. If I'd waited until I was a great writer, I'd still be writing Levi's commercials for that radio station. I couldn't do that. First, I needed the validation only publication *anywhere* could provide. Second, as the suddenly single parent of three cats, I needed money.

Validation. Money. Both are great motivators. If you are a careful writer, a driven writer, and if you can learn focus, you can start publishing now. You'll have the validation, maybe even the money. Better yet, you'll be a paid intern learning your craft as you go.

Bonnie Hearn

WHERE DO YOU START?

Give yourself permission to be a writer

Focus won't help you if you don't give yourself permission and time to write. It's really okay if your house isn't spick-and-span and if your writing matters more than a hot meal on the table every night. Why do you think God invented pizza anyway? You're a writer, and a writer doesn't have to apologize for not playing by the rules.

You've probably heard all your life that you should be well-rounded. Maybe while trying to be so, you've well-rounded yourself right into mediocrity. Work on focus. Work on honesty. Work on what you were put on earth to do. Don't worry about other people's expectations of you.

It's said that our greatest strengths are our greatest liabilities. You're loved for your honesty, loathed for your bluntness. You can't have it both ways. Don't be conned into trying to be all things to all people. Unless you're a fast-food hamburger, you'll never be loved by the masses. Don't apologize. Refuse to scatter yourself and your talents.

Be you, with every strength and flaw you possess, and that you will be reflected in your work. Your life may not read like a script from "Ozzie and Harriet," but you'll know who you are at all times. With a lot of work and a little luck, what you create will live long after the well-rounded and mass-produced have turned to dust.

Confront your fears

Many talented writers simply stop at the first draft. It wasn't as great as it felt when you wrote it; thus, it's not worth the additional work it requires.

Most beginners are afraid of failure. Many more, I think, are afraid of success. What if you actually do it? People will treat you differently. Your life will change. What will your spouse, your parents, your children say? Will you end up alone?

These are just a few of the unspoken fears writers face when dealing with fear of success. When you're truly focused, you can ignore the fear. While it may not evaporate on the spot, it will cease to control you.

Fear can't stop you if you force yourself to move on past it. No one says you have to finish a novel or win an Oscar this year. All you have to do is get started.

Invest in yourself

Sooner or later, a word processor or computer will be a necessity, if only because of how it changes your attitude toward rewriting. Postage is a major cost if you're serious about writing. You'll need to budget for those manuscripts you're sending out into the world.

You'll also need books you can mark up and use on a daily basis. You may want to enroll in a writing course or attend a seminar. Tell yourself and anyone who questions you that this is an investment in you and for you. It's your Ph.D. and deserves the same investment of money, time and work as any advanced degree in any other field of knowledge.

This doesn't mean you're going to pay anyone exorbitant amounts to critique your work, be your "agent" or publish your writing. Nor does it mean you have to be a writing-conference groupie. The major investment you must make as a writer is time. You can't pay anyone to do the work for you, and doing the work, putting your words down on paper, will take more time, more energy than any job you've ever tackled.

Write every day

It's like driving a car. You don't think much when you climb into your car, do you? You know the location of the brake pedal and how to snap yourself into the seat belts. So it is with writing. You'll be better able to focus when you practice it frequently.

When you write every day, even 15 or 30 minutes a day, you demystify the process. I've done it on my lunch hour. A horror writer friend of mine, who works as a counselor, dictates his copy while he's driving from one appointment to another. Mary Higgins Clark, who was widowed in her 30s, wrote at 5 a.m. each day before she got her children ready for school.

When you discover that writing isn't some mystical experience, you'll feel less fear, and those scribbled pieces of paper will build up. Don't worry about editing them just yet. That might stop the process.

Make the commitment to finish

Writers are finishers. They have to be. The work you submit will never be perfect. The time comes when you finally have to let go of it and seek an editorial response (translated: acceptance or rejection).

In order to get to that point, you have to rewrite, something many writers see as a chore. Think of it as a romantic relationship—heady passion and fun at the start—then damned hard work once you're into it. The temptation is always to just bail out and start over with a fresh subject.

When I interviewed the authors of "The Murder of Marilyn Monroe," which was published on the 30th anniversary of the star's death, I learned that the book was rejected 34 times. Even the house that ultimately bought the manuscript turned it down twice, once when it was submitted by an agent, once by an earlier over-the-transom submission by the writers.

Didn't they ever feel like giving up, I asked. The four women laughed. Of course, they did.

"But we made a commitment when we started that we'd meet once a week and see it through to publication," one of them said. "We knew it wasn't going to be easy."

You have to make the same commitment. You must stick with your story and your vision, if just to prove to yourself that you're capable of being a finisher. Even if you don't publish the work, you'll learn a great deal in the process of rewriting, and you'll know you're capable of more than a good start.

LEARNING TO FOCUS

When you're focused, you see past the prose on the page to the real story you're trying to tell. It's a step-by-step process at first. As you write, it becomes more spontaneous and instinctive.

Imagine you're driving through the country. Every side road has its own promise—wild flowers, perhaps, a fruit stand, a stream. If you have an idea of where you're heading, you keep driving down the road you've chosen, straight to the beach or the mountains, and you save the side roads for another trip. You can't travel every road, smell every aroma, hear every sound, experience every story in just one short drive. You've got to (1) choose your path and (2) stick to it.

The focused writer is able to reach many readers by concentrating on one reader. He or she is able to combine many ideas into a single theme. The process is as easy and as difficult as taking a photograph.

Pinpoint a publication

It can be a magazine you've read for years or a trade publication you've just encountered in Writer's Market or another reference book. In future chapters, you'll learn how to define the many types of publications and how to write to those specific markets. For now, just start thinking about the many magazines that are published and the ones that appeal to you.

Target your reader

Before you can truly focus, you have to know your reader. For whom are you writing? Don't think of a group of people. Focus on just one person with just one reason for reading what you have written. Think in terms of sex, age, goals and most important, what he or she wants from the publication.

Define your message

Good writing must serve at least one of four purposes. It must: inform, instruct, inspire or entertain. Read a minimum of three current issues of your target publication. Are the majority of the articles geared to inform, instruct, inspire or entertain? Are they how-tos, personal experience, profiles?

Now, evaluate your own article idea. Is its purpose to inform, instruct, inspire or entertain? What exactly do you want to tell the reader?

Narrow your topic

Too many beginning writers try to tell the history of the universe, yet most published articles explore specific angles, not broad topics. In journalism, we call this angle a *slant*.

When you discuss the slant of an article you're trying to sell, don't say, "It's about love." A better response is: "It's about the benefits and drawbacks of a May/December marriage." Or (to borrow the slant one of my students used): "It describes seven ways to leave your lover when he's hot and you're not."

Pretend you're a camera. If the image before you is too large, you won't be able to properly define your subject. Until you focus on a specific portion of that subject, the word picture you want to capture will be a blur. The process that limits and thus defines your story is focus.

Some writers go as far as looking through an empty toilet-paper roll to narrow and focus their stories. My students call it a Focuscope. Silly as it sounds, try looking through one of these things yourself. How much can you really see? How much of your story could you tell if you were viewing it in such a manner?

When I began writing radio commercials years ago, my cantankerous old boss, Bellman, who knew more about effective writing then than I ever will, told me to type each spot on the right side of a sheet of paper divided with a vertical line. The narrow page seemed to make it easier to cram more information into limited space.

I sometimes ask poetry students to write their poems on adding-machine tapes. This process forces them to limit their lines and their verbiage, and I hope, expand their vision. As the words are reduced, the idea is expanded.

If you don't have the infamous Focuscope, cup your hands around your eyes and pretend you are looking at your story as if aiming that imaginary camera. Not much fits within the range of your human viewfinder, but your story must.

Think "You," not "Me"

Many beginning writers focus on themselves instead of their readers. While journal writing is great, it's seldom marketable. The focus is Me when it should be You.

Someone once said that all writers began as lonely children. Because we were lonely, we read, and the act of reading led us to a love for words. If that is true, then it is ironic that we once-lonely children now find ourselves in one of life's loneliest professions. We writers need people to survive, but we must have solitude in order to create.

It is the lonely child who drives us. He wants to be heard, and this need overpowers even the fear of appearing foolish. Use the child—his need to be heard, to be read—like fuel. Let him push you into learning craft, putting your words on paper and risking rejection.

Remember, however, that no one wants to hear about your unhappy childhood or marriage, unless you can connect that experience to a universal theme. Your job is to inform, instruct, inspire or entertain. There's no room for "Poor Me" or "Wonderful Me."

In some vacant-house of a file on your computer, begin a self-indulgent journal. Call it "Story Ideas," if you like.

This journal won't keep food on the table, but it will be good company, especially before you begin publishing. You might even tap it for legitimate story ideas later on. What you can't do is confuse journal writing with writing for publication. Focus will teach you the difference.

Give yourself the gift of honesty

Almost every successful writer with whom I have worked has two qualities in common: Each is his own person, and each is (often painfully) honest.

If you can't be honest with yourself, you'll find it difficult to write with any degree of honesty. This doesn't mean you can spew out your life history on anyone within range. It does mean that you'll need personal integrity to write with conviction and to risk putting yourself on paper.

Regardless of what you write, what you *are* will show up in your work. Don't be afraid of you, what you think, feel or what you're made of.

When you master focus in your writing, you'll find it in yourself as well. The more focused and more honest your writing becomes, the more focused and honest your life will become. Focus. Honesty. They feed each other. The process may be slow, but it never stops. It's a win-win situation for you and your work.

FOCUS REVIEW

Suppose you want to write an article on some aspect of women and driving. First, **pinpoint a publication**. Your target market is a woman's magazine, let's say Woman's Day. You check Writer's Market and find that over 75 percent of the articles the magazine publishes are written by free-lancers. You note that the magazine uses articles on marriage, family life, child-rearing, education, homemaking, money management, careers, leisure activities, as well as "fresh, dramatic narratives of women's lives and concerns."

Next, you must **target your reader**. By studying copies of the magazine, you see articles such as "Where is my Twin Sister?" (personal experience), "How to Make Time for Yourself (how-to) and "12 Ways to Reduce Your Debts" (another how-to). Your reader, you discover, is a busy woman, probably with children. She needs quick information that will enhance her life.

Now it's time to **define your message and narrow your topic**. Women and driving is too broad a topic. Is your article focused to inform, instruct, inspire or entertain? You could choose to *inform* and write about women race car drivers, for instance. You might choose to *instruct* and write about how to handle road emergencies. If you choose to *inspire*, you might focus on a woman who crusades against drunk drivers. If you choose to *entertain*, you might do a first-person account of a woman learning to drive heavy equipment.

You have to ask yourself which has the greatest appeal to your target reader. You don't want the history of the universe, and you certainly don't want some Wonderful Me article on "How I Learned to Drive."

Does it sound too easy? It is, and it isn't. We all know how to focus, if we think about it. And that's the secret. Think about it.

SUMMARY

Much of what you hear about writing for publication is hocus pocus. Four of the most common misconceptions are: (1) You need an agent, (2) If you have talent, you will publish sooner or later, (3) Publishers don't want to work with beginning writers, and (4) It takes years to get published.

Bonnie Hearn

Whether you're a born writer or a taught writer, focus can improve your chances of publication. Start by giving yourself permission to be a writer and by confronting your fears, including your possible fear of success. Give yourself a budget, write every day and make a commitment to being a finisher.

Focused writing concentrates on *you*, not *me*. Its purpose is to inform, instruct, inspire or entertain. The steps are: pinpoint a publication, target your reader, define your message and narrow your topic.

ASSIGNMENT

1. Take four separate index cards or pieces of paper. On one, write INFORM. On the others, write INSTRUCT, INSPIRE and ENTERTAIN. With your target reader in mind, list possible article ideas under each heading. Pick the article idea that seems to have the greatest appeal, then write a query letter to Woman's Day or another publication that appeals to you. In the process of focusing, you may have discovered additional article ideas for other publications.

2. Visit a bookstore. Buy some magazines. Go through Writer's Market.

3. Make a list of 10 possible markets for something you'd like to write.

4. Define your reader. What do you want to tell this person?

5. Ask yourself why the editors of these publications would be interested in what you have to say. Why will your piece make the reader turn off the TV and keep on reading?

6. Go on and make your own Focuscope from an empty toilet-paper roll. Write FOCUS on it in big letters. Now try looking through it, first at the room, next at the article you envision.

Focus Your Writing

How much do you see? Is there a story there? If so, how much of the story would you tell, and where would you start it? Place the Focuscope next to your computer, typewriter or notebook.

In this chapter, we've discussed just the basics of focus. Next, we're going to examine how to use them by studying and targeting to specific publications.

CHAPTER TWO

USING FOCUS TO SECOND-GUESS THE MARKET

A former colleague of mine now works as an editor for a major fashion magazine in Singapore. When we were discussing several free-lance submissions recently, I asked for her opinion of a particular article. She looked at it briefly, then said, in the succinct manner that is her trademark, "Close, but no cigar."

In those four words, she expressed what few editors will tell you in their polite thanks-but-no-thanks letters. You've got to be better than close to get the cigar. Editors already know what best suits their publications. The job of an editor is not to find something with great potential, only something that works and that fits the publication's focus.

Don't say: "I know it's not what they usually print, but it's a wonderful idea." It may be, but if it's about the superiority of dogs, don't expect *Cat Fancy* to publish it. If your focus is holiday shopping for grandchildren, Cosmo probably won't be interested. Am I exaggerating? Not much. Are free-lancers really this off track? Many are, but you don't have to be.

FOCUS YOUR ARTICLE TO A SINGLE SENTENCE

This isn't as difficult as it sounds. If your article is focused, you should be able to reduce its theme to a sentence or two.

Start by picking up one or two copies of the publication in which you wish to publish. Don't try to bypass this very important step. You need to know your potential reader. Before you as much as look at the articles, study the table of contents, both titles and blurbs of each article.

Then, look at your own article. Can you reduce it to a grabber title and blurb? If not, work on doing just that. Don't delude yourself into thinking that the editor will understand what you mean.

Next, pretend your article is listed on that table of contents. Under which category will it fall? What will be an appropriate title? How can you describe your theme in just a few, reader-attracting words?

To understand how magazines are focused, let's dissect three publications: Writer's Digest, Motorland and Bon Appetit. First, we need to understand the types of articles each magazine publishes.

The contents page of Writer's Digest is broken down into Features, Columns and Departments. Features are obviously the best way to go. Some of the listings under that heading are:

"Avoiding The Tin Man Syndrome" by Hal Blythe and Charlie Sweet. The blurb reads: "If your characters lack heart, your writing will lack readers. But it's not difficult to bring depth to your fictional people. Here's how."

"Creating Unreliable Narrators," by William Browning Spencer. The blurb reads: "How to use narrators who are deluded, misinformed or dishonest."

FOCUSING THE ARTICLE

Subject of article _____

_____

Using the basics of focus, break down your general topic into specific article ideas

TO INFORM

1. _____
2. _____
3. _____
4. _____

TO INSTRUCT

1. _____
2. _____
3. _____
4. _____

TO INSPIRE

1. _____
2. _____
3. _____
4. _____

TO ENTERTAIN

1. _____
2. _____
3. _____
4. _____

Circle the article ideas that are most likely to appeal to the reader of this publication. Then write a query letter pitching your first choice.

Focus Your Writing

As you study the features listings, you soon begin to see how your own article can be reduced to a catchy title and a succinct blurb.

Motorland's table of contents is broken into Features and Departments, with a focus on travel. There are few blurbs, which means more extensive homework on your part. The contents page lists "Great Walks in Hong Kong." That doesn't tell you enough. When you turn to the actual story, you see: "What to do in Hong Kong After You Buy the Camcorder and Cloisonne," by Lynn Ferrin. The blurb states: "So, what did you do in Hong Kong? Hiking, mostly. *Hiking?*"

"Touring Local Factories" is also listed without a blurb. Again, you turn to the actual article. "I like work...I could watch it all day," by John Goepel. Blurb: "The process of transforming raw material into a finished product can be fascinating to see. Here are some nearby businesses that are glad to have you watch."

As it turns out, the blurb is also the lead to a list article profiling manufacturing companies that welcome tourists.

Bon Appetit has a lovely layout, down to and including its features. Headings are Food, Entertaining & the Home, Travel & Restaurants, The World of Bon Appetit and Cooking with Bon Appetit. Titles are short, and blurbs are focused to the luscious theme of the publication.

"Oktoberfest!" by Betty Rosbottom. Blurb: "Great food for an autumn tradition, from sausages with caramelized onions to spiced pear and sour cherry strudels."

"Barbecue, Argentine Style," by Tricia Callas. Blurb: "A visiting polo team joins a Maryland family feast."

With a little study and a little more practice, you will be able to focus your article to a specific publication by creating a title and blurb similar to the ones the publication uses. This is the way I sold my own piece about how to end an article to Writer's Digest.

On the manuscript, right under the title ("The Last Word"), I typed the blurb, which ultimately appeared in the magazine:

Bonnie Hearn

There's more than one way to end an article. Here are six proven ending types guaranteed to successfully conclude almost any story.

The next step is to focus your language to the publication. The blurb was just a start. Sooner or later, you must actually write that article.

Study the articles within the publication of your choice. What words come up again and again? Find the article closest to yours and circle the power words.

Marketing people have understood for years that you can instantly establish empathy by using the same terminology and speech patterns as someone else. If you plant a few of these power words into your text, the editor will be more likely to feel a kinship with you. That's all you want or need at this point.

Studying, not just reading, the publication to which you wish to submit will teach you more than any market listing in a writers' magazine. You'll get a feel for what type of leads the publication uses, the length of its pieces and the values of its target readers. You will also learn whether to use *said* or *says*, whether to address sources by first or last names as well as the overall *tone* of the magazine, be it formal, chatty or academic.

You'll be able to use this information, as well as all or part of your blurb, when you prepare a query letter to market your article.

Will this kill your originality? It shouldn't. Your voice, your style will make your work not just a paint-by-number piece.

In "Make Your Words Work," a book I recommend, Gary Provost said, "The writing that has worked in the past is an enormous body of evidence we can sift through for clues to good writing. The successful writers of today, the ones who are getting published and cashing checks, are those who recognize what made someone else's writing work."

Most editors will never get to the bottom of that slush pile on the desk (or, in my case, those *piles,* plural, of manuscripts lining the room). We reach in, hope, reject; reach in, hope again, reject, only until we fill that issue with manuscripts that work. It makes

Focus Your Writing

me crazy to open a promising envelope and pull out fiction and poetry, which our newspaper never publishes, or an article of 9,000 words, regardless of its quality. Such submissions waste my time, the writer's time and give free-lancers a bad name.

Why throw away your postage? If you take the time to read the magazine, you'll be ahead of many free-lancers competing with you for a sale. If you go beyond that and study the focus of the magazine, you'll be able to second-guess the publication and the editor to whom you hope to sell.

Sure, it would be easier to send out copies of "Wonderful Me From A to Z" to every publication in Writer's Market, but unless you're Madonna or Bill Clinton, you probably won't find a home for it. If you want the cigar, do this important homework before you write a single word.

SUMMARY

If it is to sell, your article can't just come close to what the publication buys. Its subject, tone and language must reflect the focus of that publication.

Reduce your article to a single sentence. Look at the table of contents and imagine how your article's title and blurb would read if they were printed there.

Study the language of the published articles and structure your own article accordingly. Pay attention to length, lead types and style. By studying the focus of your intended market before you write the article, you'll save both your time and the time of the editor to whom you're submitting.

ASSIGNMENT

1. Buy four magazines in which you'd like to publish. Study the table of contents in each and note how blurbs are written.

2. Write sample titles and blurbs for an article or articles you would like to sell. Target the blurbs to each of the four publications.

3. Test yourself. Which titles and blurbs would fit into the contents pages of the publications you have selected? Which do not fit?

Now that you're learning how to target an idea to the market, you need to know how to put these basic principles to work by coming up with fast-track tips to publication. It all begins with an idea.

Focus Your Writing

CHAPTER THREE

IDEAS THAT SELL (AND WHO BUYS THEM)

I once attended a writers' club meeting where a visitor announced that although he was not a writer, he would be willing to split with any of us what we earned from writing his ideas, of which he had many.

We groaned in unison, and the poor man was bewildered. He didn't understand that ideas are everywhere. The problem is not where to get an idea, but which idea.

Editors don't wade through the slush pile because we enjoy it. We depend on fresh ideas and new voices. While we might purchase fiction from established writers, we know that the content of an article is more important than the name recognition of the author.

Should you write what you know? Sure. At least, you'd better know about it by the time you sit down to write. More important than what you know is what interests you. Few can write with conviction on a subject they care nothing about. Once you start focusing on ideas, you'll find yourself interested in topics you never before considered.

Focus Your Writing

I began writing seriously in the early 1970s while I was employed as a copywriter for a successful rock-radio station. I was young, had no contacts and not the slightest idea how to break in. Writer's Market reported that trade magazines were easy markets for beginners, but what did I know about business, chain-store management or something as foreign as western retailing?

Actually, a great deal, I discovered. Some western retailers in our city advertised on radio, with positive results. I tailored a query on how to increase sales through radio commercials and sent that query off to 10 target publications.

The first article sold to Western Outfitter magazine, where it was published in two parts. Could it be that easy? Of course not. A subsequent article about our computerized radio station was nastily rejected by the editor of a secretarial magazine (no longer in business, I'm happy to report). The editor did offer me a $15 "finder's fee."

After considerable anguish, I decided I was a writer, not a finder, and I forced myself to send out the article again. It sold to the nasty editor's competition for $75, a decent trade-magazine fee in those days.

After that first setback, both my craft and my luck improved with every piece. I went from a would-be to a published writer, not Shakespeare, not Joan Didion, but a published writer nevertheless. My focus (although I didn't call it that back then) was to build a body of credits, something I could list in query letters to other publications. It's easier than you think. Once you've sold, editors tend to take you seriously.

A writing professor I respect tells his students to ignore smaller markets.

"If you start small, you'll stay small," he tells them. "Go for the big markets."

He's right, if you happen to be the reincarnation of Raymond Carver, **and** if you happen to connect with a good editor on a good day. What I think he forgets, possibly because he is both gifted and successful, is that most writers need validation to keep them going.

"So, you're a writer," your friends ask. "What have you published?"

Unlike the successful professor, you mutter, "Well, I'm working on a few things."

Writing is intimidating enough. Some of us already feel pretty weird spending time and money, not to mention our hearts and souls, for something that may be a crazy dream. Don't sell out the dream for the validation, but don't sacrifice the validation for the dream. There is no reason you can't have both.

WHERE TO FIND IDEAS

Your daily newspaper is a good source of ideas that might have a national slant. Many of my national sales have been with local subjects other writers overlooked. One woman I interviewed founded a successful wheelchair-manufacturing company in our city after a hang-gliding accident left her a paraplegic. She then started Winners on Wheels, a national nonprofit organization much like scouting, for children with disabilities.

After my local article was published, I queried Family Circle, which purchased "Winner On Wheels." How many similar outstanding people do you read about in your own community newspaper? When you do so, stop and focus on the subject's national potential. What publications would be interested in such a piece?

Even television shows such as "Hard Copy" and "Inside Edition" get their ideas from local newspapers. Industry R & D Inc. (6565 Sunset Blvd. Hollywood, California 90028) collects faxed stories from free-lancers around the country and publishes the best in a tip sheet for a list of subscribers that includes "America's Most Wanted," "Entertainment Tonight" and major wire services. While it costs the writer nothing to submit, the compensation for a local story selected for national exposure can be lucrative.

Some writers keep a file of local articles they hope to one-day pursue. To me, that's a bit like clipping recipes you hope to prepare when you find the time. You end up with great intentions and folders of yellowed newspaper. If that recipe is more appealing than the Lean Cuisine in the freezer, you'll prepare it tonight, even if you have to make an extra trip to the grocery store for pine nuts and fresh basil. If the local story really strikes you, stop right now, tear it out (your mate will understand) focus on a market and have a query in tomorrow's mail.

Your chamber of commerce directory will give you an idea of the major businesses and industries in your community that might lend themselves to wider coverage in a trade or consumer magazine. Heads of local clubs and organizations would just love to talk to someone who is writing an article.

That's how ideas hatch. Research. Contacts. Not some poignant reflection on the meaning of life.

SEASONAL OR EVERGREEN?

What articles sell best? That depends on the market. Some writers prefer what they call the "evergreen" article that an editor can use at any time. Seasonal articles often offer beginners a chance to break in.

Holidays, if you can bear to think about them six months before they arrive, are a natural focus for articles. I never receive enough good Christmas material, a complaint I've heard from many other editors. One of my students sold her first piece to Christian Parent. The article, which listed ways to include grandparents in family activities, was published, as the writer suggested, to coincide with Grandparents' Day.

Another student wrote about how she coped with the death of her father (a tricky subject and not one I recommend for beginners). The writer described putting on one of her father's

Pendleton shirts, which after 10 years, she still wore every time she needed a hug.

She submitted the story to our newspaper for the Father's Day issue. It was purchased and published, along with a photo of the author in her father's shirt.

WHAT PUBLICATIONS BUY

The magazine market can be broken into two categories: consumer and trade publications.

Consumer publications range from photography, religious and science magazines, to women's, teens and ethnic publications. Trade magazines provide information to those in various business, technical and professional fields, ranging from beverage and bottling, to construction and real estate. Within these broad categories, lurk several sub-categories of special interest to the serious writer.

Trade Magazines

These gems are truly the hidden articles market. Every industry, from retail stores to advertising, has at least one. Their editors tend to buy: how-to articles, that show a single aspect of how someone in the industry is successful; marketing articles, that demonstrate how to better sell products; personal-experience articles, that tell, in the first-person how "I" did it. These can also be as-told-to articles.

Sometimes trade editors buy nostalgia articles about the industry. Often they publish personal profiles of people who have made it. They almost always prefer an upbeat, clean and strictly business format with lots of quotes. What to remember here is that your reader wants to learn something positive and beneficial as a result of reading your article.

Focus Your Writing

Consumer Magazines

These are harder to crack, because the money is better than it is for trade magazine articles. If you want to break into consumer publications, you have to do it with an article only you can write. That means you have to have an exclusive source or an irresistible idea.

Many consumer magazines publish monthly columns that are especially receptive to free-lance submissions. Study them. What/whom do you know that would serve as the basis of a short article?

As a rule, consumer magazine editors buy: celebrity profile pieces, how-tos from qualified sources, disease-of-the-week stories about people who have overcome illness and health problems, and occasionally, profiles of real people who have made a difference.

City and Regional Magazines

These publications fall in the consumer magazine category, and they are an excellent market for free-lancers.

If you're going to write for a city/regional magazine, you have to have a feel for the lifestyle of the people who live in that city or region. You have to know where to go, what to do and why sushi bars are hot, and computer dating is not.

These magazines are trendy. The activities, people and food that were big news yesterday might now be as dated as black-bean lasagna. Trendy isn't the only way to break in, however. An effective alternative is the historical piece.

While researching a newspaper article on wine country, I fell in love with California's Napa Valley and the glossy, gorgeous Napa Valley Appellation magazine published there. No way could I fake enough knowledge of wine to write even an intelligent query.

Quite by accident (if you believe in accidents), I came upon a book on "ghost" wineries that had ceased operation at the turn of the century. I talked to the editor of the magazine, who (another "accident") was looking for a piece about deserted wineries that had been refurbished and reestablished by a new breed of winemaker. The result was my article "Ghost Stories," which profiled three of these wineries.

Travel Magazines

These consumer magazines are also receptive to free-lancers. If you're planning a trip to China, write a few query letters about your projected piece before you go. Remember to focus your query. Don't say, "I'm planning a trip to China and wonder if you'd like me to write something for your magazine while I'm there."

Travel magazine editors like to know the who, what, when, where and how of your trip. They don't like, "My First Visit To France." Dig deeper. Tell about the big balloon festival or jazz-fest in your community, or show readers how they can visit Mexico on a few pesos a day.

Pay for travel articles can keep you in plane tickets. I received $450 for my 1,500-word winery piece with the option to sell it again six months after publication. Islands (3886 State Street, Santa Barbara, CA) which is 95-percent free-lance written, pays expenses and $800 to $3,000 for assigned articles of 2,000 to 4,000 words. Side Streets of the World (Holland & Edwards Publishing, 250 Mercer St. NY, NY 10012) is 90-percent free-lance written and pays $2,500 and expenses to published writers who have distinguished themselves in some type of writing other than travel.

Close to 200 travel newsletters, sold to subscribers for around $75 a year, are published in this country. Many buy free-lance articles that tell everything good, bad and ugly a traveler needs to know about a specific destination. Pay is around 50 cents a word.

Focus Your Writing

General-Interest Publications

A general-interest publication is what the Saturday Evening Post was at its best, something the family can read, a "Sixty Minutes" in print. With the popularity of what is known as "niche marketing," most publications today are tightly focused to a specific audience.

Some general-interest publications still manage to survive, including the grand daddy Readers Digest. Before you send off your brainchild there, be aware that anyone who can scribble his/her name has done the same, usually without success.

The RD editors I have met are encouraging and accessible. Many speak at writing conferences, and like most editors, really do want to find new talent. Their problem is the avalanche of submissions they receive, many of which are not targeted to their needs.

Lesser known general-interest publications include The American Legion Magazine, which is 95-percent free-lance written, or Friendly Exchange, which is 80-percent free-lance written. You'll find submission requirements for these and more in the current Writer's Market.

Newspapers

Your local newspaper may be the best home for your first article. The features department of your paper is a good place to start.

Because they're improperly addressed, many submissions never make it to the right editor's desk. Don't be afraid to query via letter or even phone call, and never, never, never address anything but a letter to "Editor."

Profiles also fare well in newspapers. If you know of someone in your city who is doing something newsworthy, write or phone the appropriate editor (usually the features or business editor) and test the water.

Also products of niche marketing, newspapers are broken into sections designed to attract specific readers. The "women's pages" of yesteryear are alive and well and living under euphemisms such as "Tempo" or "Style." Teen and senior news is published in one section, at least weekly, by many papers. Minority and Generation X pieces are welcomed and even sought out by a growing number of newspaper editors aware of the importance of diversity.

Literary Magazines

Although the pay is minuscule, these are excellent markets for book reviews and essays, not to mention poetry and fiction. As with any publication, do your homework and study several issues of the magazine before you submit. Don't just send your creation off to the Paris Review because it's the only name you recognize.

I once served as a national writing contest judge with a Paris Review editor, who told me that not even the winning manuscripts came close to what she was seeking. Imagine how her slush pile must look, and do consider submitting to less-known but respected publications such as Amelia, which publishes articles, essays, reviews and poetry. Poets & Writers magazine is an excellent source for literary markets.

THE BIG TWELVE

These articles are probably the easiest to sell to today's market.

1. How to

Whether it's about making button covers or coping with a serious illness, the focused how-to article will almost always find a market.

2. Personal experience

If you or someone you interview had an experience you can dramatize as an article that will demonstrate a universal truth, the personal-experience format may work for you. Many women's magazines buy such articles.

3. Profile

Whether a successful entrepreneur or an entertainer, interesting people are usually the stuff of which equally interesting articles are made. Many of my students have made their first sales with profiles.

4. Disease of the week

With the right slant, articles about overcoming and dealing with illness are highly marketable. Focus is especially important here.

5. Travel

Many general-interest publications include travel articles. The ideal one may be in your own backyard. What events make your area of the country worth visiting? Can experts in your city provide you with tips that would benefit the readers of your target publication?

An unusual slant was used by one writer who told of meeting an American-born Italian in Italy. The writer, an American-born Armenian, wrote a personal-experience travel article titled, "My Feet Don't Touch the Ground," which sold to an Armenian literary magazine.

The writer's family had been murdered in the Armenian massacre of 1915. His theme was that he traveled, not to find his roots as the Italian did, but because he had no real home and no roots to discover.

6. Nostalgia

The good old days, whether the 1930s, 1940s, '50s or even the '60s, make good copy, if you can involve the reader in the experience and evoke the smell, taste and feel of times past. With nostalgia articles, try to focus on the experience and avoid the "Times-were-better-then" approach.

7. Essay or personal opinion

A small but steady market exists for personal-opinion pieces, and newspapers are just one. The greatest reason most of these articles fail is the writer's inability to convey his/her beliefs, however controversial, to paper.

A second reason is that subject matter and style are too similar to what the publication is already buying from national columnists. Be original. Be honest, and develop a thick skin.

8. Review

This is another area where you must be willing to commit on paper. Many newspapers and some magazines buy free-lance restaurant and book reviews. While the pay is not great, reviews are an excellent way to polish your craft, if you can deal with the repercussions of putting your opinions in print.

My favorite restaurant reviewer was devastated when after bashing a local pub for serving flavorless food, she received a load of hate mail from the restaurant's fans and a 50-pound salt block from its owner. "But I just told the truth," she said. Yes, to 350,000 readers, not all of whom agreed with her.

A retired nurse received a phone call from a local hospital after she'd trashed, with great humor and nastiness, its new policy of referring to nurses as "wellness facilitators." The call, from a top administrator, turned out to be an offer for a consulting job, translated, a paid position in return for being more wellness-facilitator-friendly in future editorials. She politely declined.

Would the nurse, the restaurant reviewer, write those same articles again? Of course. They've learned that when you put your opinions in print, you must be ready for those who ignore Mark Twain's advice to never do battle with someone who has more ink than you.

9. Humor

A market for the humorous article always exists, but it takes a special gift to be funny. It also takes the ability to look honestly at yourself without blindly poking fun at someone or something else.

Humor writing also benefits from a universal subject. A writer I met at a conference and later purchased free-lance articles from made her first big sale with a humor piece.

"Kleptomaniac Cat," sold to Good Housekeeping for $1,500. When I read it, I instantly thought of my own cat, who steals and hides empty tuna cans.

The writer's success is an illustration of focus. She took the large subject of cats and focused it down to that universal, humorous cat-owner experience: discovering your cat's a thief.

10. Trend

Whether it's the move away from alcohol or the self-aware male of the '90s, an emerging trend is solid article material.

Robert Bly's wonderful book, "Iron John," is credited with spawning the current men's movement. You don't have to be Robert Bly, and you don't have to create the trend, however. Imagine how many articles, profiles, interviews, essays and even humorous articles (about men running naked in the woods) have been written as a result of that single trend.

11. Cooking/Recipes

With the cocooning of America, cooking at home is receiving increased attention, and not just in food magazines.

People are more interested in food and its history, not only in collections of recipes.

For the writer who can spot the trends and reveal the history of what we eat in an interesting manner, food is one of the most marketable topics around.

12. New Age

The '60s (which lasted until about the mid-1970s) dealt with independence. The issue in the '70s was taking care of No. 1. The '80s heralded a return to materialism. Many believe the years that follow will be more spiritual and less materialistic. How to heal yourself, your relationship or your life, including the use of spiritualism, astrology and the power of the mind, will be important topics of the future, many say.

You don't have to have the answers, but you need to seek out people who do. I know little about feng shui (the Eastern practice of arranging mirrors, crystals, wind chimes and furniture to create good energy in a room), but I published an article based on interviews with several feng shui experts.

Other writers I respect are currently researching such topics as past lives, out-of-body experiences and UFOs, subjects they might not have touched in the '80s.

Test your idea before you write.

Go through your publication of choice. Define the types of articles therein. How are they constructed? Study the leads, the way pertinent information is woven into the article, the use of dialogue, if any, and the conclusion. Your article should be constructed in a similar manner.

Before you write the article or even the query letter for it, ask yourself the following:

Is the subject overworked?

Has it already been done to death in magazines and/or books?

Is the subject too personal?

Why you named your cat Petunia might be too personal, even for a pet magazine. An article on popular names for cats and the categories into which they fall did sell to Cat Fancy magazine.

Are you speaking to the publication's target reader?

An article on second marriages is obviously not right for Seventeen. That doesn't mean Seventeen hasn't received a few.

Is your article too preachy?

Most beginning writers with a cause generalize instead of focus. Why abortion is Right with a capital R or Wrong with a capital W is of little interest to anyone but the writer.

Is your focus too narrow?

Publications need to appeal to a wide readership. An esoteric piece on Shakespeare would probably be out of place in Writer's Digest, for instance. A filler article on phrases from Shakespeare that became titles for books might work.

Is your slant fresh?

The fresher the slant, the better chance you have of selling. Try to make the reader look at an old topic in a new way.

Take the subject of aging, for instance. When properly focused and slanted, it becomes fresh. "35 and Over the Hill?" was published by Redbook magazine, and "Beauty and the Late Bloomer" was published by the now-defunct Lear's. Each had a different slant and a different audience.

Be tough on yourself. Pretend you're an editor evaluating your query letter. Is your article fresh and focused enough to make that editor decide to publish it?

SUBJECTS TO AVOID

Certain topics are overdone by many beginning writers. The biggest taboo is trying to be too heavy-handed.

As part of my advanced writing class, students produce a literary magazine that is published by the school. Craig, my supervisor, ultimately decides what will go in and what will not.

"They're all about death," he complained when he read the first batch of submissions. "Can't beginning writers do anything else?"

Craig had a point, one I had never considered until we had that conversation.

Beginning writers want to be deep, tragic and profound. We all do. It's easier. You, however, want to sell. Believe me, a fresh idea will do that faster than death and destruction, which is best left in the hands of more experienced writers.

For nine years, I coordinated our newspaper's Holiday Memories essay contest. I'm ashamed to tell you how sick I got of what we called "dead-grandfather stories." The poor form actually hardened us to the genuine emotions and experiences the writers were attempting to share.

Write your dead-grandfather story, your unhappy-childhood story and your miserable-marriage story, if you still want to, after you're Pat Conroy. Or keep a journal and focus your working writing on what you want to publish now.

SUMMARY

Your daily newspaper is an excellent source for article ideas for national publication. Chambers of commerce and heads of professional organizations can provide you with information for trade and consumer articles.

Evergreen articles can be used by an editor at any time. Submit seasonal articles months in advance.

Consumer magazines serve the general public. Trade magazines serve various industries. The pay is less than for consumer articles, and the opportunities for free-lancers are often greater.

Consumer publications fall into various types. In addition to well-known men's, women's and teens' publications, are city and regional magazines, travel magazines, general-interest publications, newspapers and literary magazines.

Focus Your Writing

The Big Twelve article types selling today are: how-to, personal experience, profile, disease of the week, travel, nostalgia, essay/personal opinion, review, humor, trend, cooking and New Age.

Before you write, ask yourself if your subject is overworked, too personal or too sentimental. Be certain you are speaking to the publication's target reader and that your article isn't too preachy. Check for a too-narrow focus. The fresher the slant, the better your chance.

ASSIGNMENT

1. Go back to your list of publications, trade, consumer or both, for which you would like to write. Make a list of the types of articles they contain, using the Big Twelve as a reference.

2. Come up with an article idea for each one. It can be the same idea with a different slant. Next to each idea, note into which of the Big Twelve categories it falls.

3. If you've already written an article, analyze it. Does it fall into one of the Big Twelve categories, or does it drift into Poor Me or Wonderful Me? Is it a real article or a journal entry? Can you salvage it and target it to a specific publication?

At this point, you should have several marketable article ideas. You should also have several target publications in mind. But where do you begin? With the lead, of course. Those first two or three paragraphs are the most important part of your article. In the next chapter, you'll learn which ones really work and which ones mark you as an amateur.

Bonnie Hearn

CHAPTER FOUR

FOCUS YOUR LEAD/FOCUS YOUR STORY

Plato said, "The beginning is the most important part of the work." This is especially true today, when many editors won't read past a weak lead. Those first few words you write must telegraph both the tone and the focus of your article. Above all, they must *hook* the reader, not to mention the editor.

How do you find the right hook? That depends on the publication to which you are submitting and the reader you are attempting to engage.

THE 3 P's—*PROMISE, PROOF, PAYOFF*

Of the many leads and lead combinations available, here are five that will rarely fail you: The Case History Lead, the Shocking Statement Lead, the Theme Lead, the Anecdote Lead and maybe even the Scenic Lead.

When these leads work, they must be more than just good prose. They should be short, no more than three, maybe four brief paragraphs, and *they have to make a promise to the reader.*

THE 3 P's

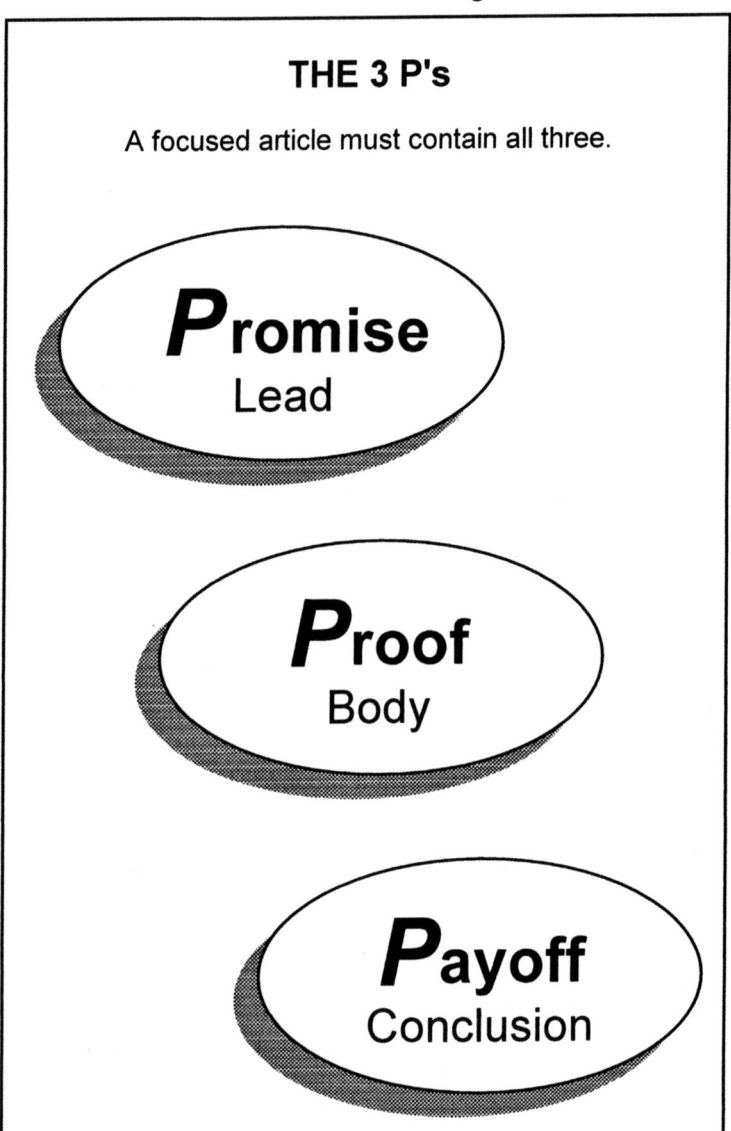

A focused article must contain all three.

Promise
Lead

Proof
Body

Payoff
Conclusion

The promise is followed by proof and payoff. The 3 P's, promise, proof and payoff, are what focus your story.

If you're having problems focusing, those problems could be rooted in a weak or too-long lead. Once you have the right lead for the story you want to tell, the rest will follow. The right lead can indeed lead you to the article you are trying to write. In journalism, it's who, what, when, where, why and how, the **Summary Lead**.

Use journalistic leads only if you're writing for a newspaper or a publication that uses a journalistic approach. The purpose of newspaper leads is to shoot the information out there to as many potential readers as possible before they turn the page.

Because magazine articles are longer, as a rule, and because their readers are more narrow in focus, magazine writers can get away with a more relaxed approach but not too relaxed.

Many books have been written on all the clever leads the writer can use to "hook" a reader. Many of these leads simply don't work, perhaps because the writers forget that you don't just hook your reader. You have to reel him in, too.

The Question Lead is my least favorite.

Did you know you can lose weight by increasing your water consumption?

"No. So what? Where's the TV Guide, Mabel?"

You ask a question, the reader answers it and goes on with the rest of his life. A journalism professor I know tells his students that they can use the Question Lead only after they turn 35.

Since most of his students are under 20, I think he's saying that a reporter needs at least 15 years of experience before he or she has enough knowledge to accurately judge when a Question Lead will work.

Even if you opt for a Question Lead, think carefully before you begin it with: *Did you know...?*

Now, let's try writing the same information with a **Case History Lead**.

Focus Your Writing

Joe Blow was 40 pounds overweight three years ago. Today he looks younger and has energy he never knew he possessed. The secret is water, lots of it.

"Turn off the TV, Mabel. I'm trying to read."

The Case History Lead tells us at once that one man, Joe Blow, lost a bunch of weight just by drinking water. The lead is your promise. The proof is comprised of your supporting quotes and facts. The payoff is when you show the reader how he or she can do the same.

The Shocking Statement Lead is powerful, as long as you can back it up with proof and payoff.

What some medical experts now believe to be the easiest and most effective way to lose weight and keep it off costs only a few cents a day and is as close as your kitchen sink.

A fine example of this lead is in "Barbara's Backlash," an article about the former First Lady written by Marjorie Williams in Vanity Fair.

Even Barbara Bush's stepmother is afraid of her. Over the course of a half-hour interview, Willa Pierce, the South Carolina painter the First Lady's widowed father married in 1952, hasn't commented on anything much more controversial than her famous stepdaughter's shoe size. But now, in a quavering voice, she is re-evaluating her decision to say anything at all.

The Theme Lead is used in many personal-opinion pieces.

Bonnie Hearn

> *The new water diet proves once more how much baloney the public is willing to swallow in its interminable search for the fountain of youth.*

In the Theme Lead, you just state your opinion (promise), which you will follow with your proof and payoff.

> *Youth isn't wasted on the young. Sammy Cahn was wrong about that. The young need youth. They'd be nothing without it.*

This is the Theme Lead Susan Rieger wrote for "Beauty and the Late Bloomer" in Lear's.

Another option is the **Anecdote Lead**. You create a story that becomes the symbol of the theme of your article. These are tricky leads, but they work well with essays and dramatic pieces.

Sabine Morrow landed her restaurant-reviewing job at our newspaper because of a sample review she wrote about an out-of-the-way Italian restaurant that delivered far more than its location promised. Here's how she did it.

> *You've heard the story. A single woman in New York City can't find Mr. Right. She jets to Dubrovnik, where she meets the man of her dreams, who is, it turns out, also from New York. They even live in the same apartment building.*
>
> *You guessed it. He was right under her nose all the time.*
>
> *This also holds true if you're looking for a restaurant serving fine Italian cuisine, expertly prepared seafood and professional service.*
>
> *Look no farther than Peppino's. This gem of a restaurant, housed in what once was an Original Joe's wannabe, is serving up authentic Italian food to savvy locals.*

Focus Your Writing

Morrow didn't stop there. After a glowing review of the restaurant's fare, she ended with her theme:

> *It's hard to find fault with Peppino's, except perhaps its location. On that busy corner, overshadowed by Tor Nino's and Circuit City, you don't expect to find one of the best Italian restaurants around, but then who would have thought you could find love in Dubrovnik?*

This doesn't mean that you need to refer back to your lead in your last paragraph. As you'll soon discover, how you end is as important as how you begin. The lead has its own purpose. It's your proof, and you'll often have better results when you choose a different payoff.

Let's try the Anecdote Lead with our water article.

> *Joe Blow walked into his house and reached for his favorite beverage, not the calorie-ridden cola, not even the Perrier. Joe turned on the faucet and filled his glass with the one substance that stood between him and the obesity that had plagued him for 20 years.*

Remember that the lead must be followed by proof and payoff if it is to be successful. Little will kill your article faster than a Anecdote Lead that doesn't work. If your lead truly does not represent the theme of your article, try another.

Many writers, especially travel writers, swear by the **Scenic Lead**, usually a short description of a locale or a certain food, or in the case of this example from Fredric Koeppel, Scripps Howard News Service, the taste of a fine cabernet.

> *For '92, Beringer winemaker Ed Sbragia fashioned a 100 percent enticing bouquet of*

mint, minerals, oak, vanilla and intense berry scents. In the mouth, the wine displays polished tannins and suave oak, a chewy texture, deep rich raspberry and black currant flavors and exquisite balance.

In the hands of a writer as skilled as Koeppel, it works. The Scenic Lead is not a favorite of mine, possibly because it's one many beginners who submit to our newspaper execute poorly.

They often remind me of what William Zinsser says about travel writing in "On Writing Well," a book you should own.

"Travelese is a land 'where old meets new.' I'm amazed at the number of places where old meets new. Old never meets old. The meeting occurs in the 'twisting alleys' and 'bustling thoroughfares' of storied Tangier or picturesque Zanzibar. This is terrain dotted with 'byways,' usually half-forgotten or at least hidden. It's a world where inanimate objects spring to transitive life: storefronts smile, buildings boast, ruins beckon and the very chimney tops sing their immemorial song of welcome."

The best of the Scenic Leads create sensory impressions so intriguing that the reader wants to ride along. A long, leisurely lead sets the tone for Gene Bourg's article, "Don't Call it 'Cajun,'" which appeared in Saveur.

It is a damp autumn night just outside Lafayette, Louisiana. On the bare wooden bandstand at Randol's Restaurant, the accordion takes up the double-time beat of the washboard and guitar. As fiddle bow scrapes against catgut, the singer steps up to the microphone. From the depths of his thorax comes what

Focus Your Writing

> *sounds like either a primal cry of ecstasy or a howl of pain. "Oh-yiiiy!" he cries against the music. "Oh-yiiiy!"*

The lead continues for two more paragraphs, describing the dancers, the room, the food.

> *Together, this food, this music, and these dancers, undulating counterclockwise around the floor like some unstoppable force of nature, form a kind of gumbo of their own,* he writes.

The **Quote Lead** is another favorite of beginners.

> *"Another glass of water, please."*
>
> *It's Joe Blow's drink of choice, his secret to weight loss.*

Quote Leads tend to sound contrived. They try to be fiction and attempt to make what follows more important than it is. As a result, they set up too many expectations in the reader.

A Quote Lead can work when a well-known person is the one being quoted, and if that person's name is introduced early in the lead. You may also want to use one if you have a really shocking or ironic quote. Still, at least consider using that quote at the end of your piece instead of at the beginning.

Two others, the Imperative Lead and the Direct Address Lead, are favorites of many newspaper feature writers.

The Imperative Lead instructs the reader to do something.

> *Try this restaurant. You'll like it.*

The Direct Address Lead speaks directly to the reader.

Bonnie Hearn

So you want to lose that extra 20 pounds you've been carrying around for far too long. Water could be the answer.

Where have you heard that language before? That's right. In those dreaded television commercials. Because this is the language of advertising copy, it can make an article sound like a commercial, especially if the focus is a specific product or service. For the right story, they can be effective, but the beginner should be careful with them.

Another lead to avoid at first is the **All-That-Glitters-is-Not-Gold Lead**. This clever-on-the-outside device employs a well-known phrase, such as, "All that glitters is not gold," or a line from a poem in an attempt to lend importance to the story. Often it's too much of a stretch, and the lead conjures memories that are not related to the piece.

Water, water everywhere, and not a drop to drink is not the case for those who are serious about losing weight and keeping it off.

While the lead almost works, almost is not enough for the focused writer. If you start a piece with something like: *This is the way the world ends...not with a bang, but a whimper*, you'll set up some pretty high expectations in your reader, and you'd better be prepared to follow the lead with something as good as T.S. Eliot's famous line.

The Gimmick Lead seldom works, primarily because it tends to focus the reader's attention on the writer instead of the subject.

Water, clean, refreshing, clear-as-crystal water. You bathe in it. You swim in it. You wash your car with it. On occasion, you even drink it. Now, you may be able to lose weight with it.

Focus Your Writing

An example is the lead from "A Good Politician—Period," by Eugene Kennedy, which ran in Chicago Times magazine.

> *Harold Washington is Chicago's Everyman, embodying and reflecting lofty dreams and deep angers; a man whose eyes, sewn almost as shut as a dead man's by his expansive grin, give off ambiguous light—now twinkling, now glittering—in a face, smooth here and pitted there, that, as much a coat of arms as Mayor Daley's, reveals and sums him up: planes and creases hinting at lightning intelligence, sluggard hipness, a preacher's courtliness and cunning, a gambler's been-to-the-bank-and-back charm, an insinuation of intimacy, winking conspiratorially at a street-smart youth or nudging a beaming banker's arm above fine linen and silver.* It goes on.

With a gifted writer, such a lead may find its way to print. This one did. It also appeared in an article as an example of how to write effective leads. True, it's original, and it contains some colorful images. My objections are that it's not focused, it draws more attention to the writer than the subject, and it intimidates the reader. Be honest. Weren't you glad when it finally ended?

If the Gimmick Lead is to work, it must promise you enough that you're willing to keep reading in search of the ultimate payoff. One that accomplishes that for me is by Jim Detjen, Knight-Ridder Newspapers, in a syndicated book review of "GENIUS: The Life and Science of Richard Feynman, by James Gleick.

> *Circle the correct answer:*
> *Richard Feynman was (a) a bongo player, (b) a safecracker, (c) a marijuana smoker, (d) a patron of topless bars, (e) all of the above.*

Now, answer the following:

Richard Feynman was: (a) a key developer of the atomic bomb, (b) a Nobel Prize-winning scientist, (c) a legendary physics teacher, (d) a caustic member of the commission investigating the space shuttle Challenger disaster, (e) all of the above.

The answer to both questions is "e."

Both of the above leads were written about remarkable people. The first lead dazzles, but, I think it dazzles a little too much. It almost pushes you away. The second lead pulls you along and makes you want to know more about this man who is "all of the above." Any Gimmick Lead you create must do the same.

As you write, you'll discover the leads that work for you. Which is right for your story? Trust yourself. What seems right for what you want to say? Effective writing communicates. It's you talking to just one other person—not tap dancing, not preaching a sermon.

A poet/professor once told me that good writing comes, not from the head, but from the gut. Listen to your gut. Feel your story there and write accordingly.

SUMMARY

The right lead will indeed lead you to the story you want to tell. Five that will rarely fail you are: the Case History Lead, the Shocking Statement Lead, the Theme Lead, the Anecdote Lead and (in the right hands) the Scenic Lead.

The lead is your promise to the reader. The promise is followed by proof and payoff. The 3 P's, promise, proof and payoff, focus your story.

Leads that are more difficult to pull off include: the Question Lead and the Quote Lead. Because the Imperative Lead and the

Focus Your Writing

Direct Address Lead incorporate the language of advertising, they can come across as commercials.

The All-That-Glitters-Is-Not-Gold Lead depends on a famous phrase or quotation that may overshadow the rest of the piece or be too much of a stretch.

The Gimmick Lead, which can dazzle, often dazzles too much and focuses the reader's attention on the writer and not the subject of the piece.

Experimenting with different types of leads and following your instincts will help you begin to create beginnings that truly lead the reader to the proof and payoff of your story.

ASSIGNMENT

1. Write a lead for the article you want to write. Tell it from the gut. Make it short, succinct, focused.

2. Take the same story. Try it with different leads. Which feels best to you? Which makes you want to write more?

3. Buy some highlighter pens, at least four of them. Get a newspaper and a couple of magazines. Go through and highlight the leads in one color. This is your promise. Try to identify each lead by type. Which ones work best?

4. Next, take a second highlighter pen. Go through each article and try to identify the proof. How does the writer make his point? This is usually the bulk of the article.

5. Now, take a third highlighter pen and find the payoff. How does the writer do it? Does the conclusion connect with the lead? How does it pay off that initial promise?

6. Finally, take that fourth pen and highlight the last paragraph of each article. What does that last paragraph add, if

anything? Is it just filling space, or is it part of the payoff? Don't toss out the pens after this exercise. Wait until you read an article that really touches you and outline it in the same manner.

Be warned that you may never been able to read the same after you've learned to read for focus. Consider it the price you pay for being a writer.

Now that you know how to focus your lead, you're ready to interview the subject of the article you're writing. In the next chapter, you'll learn four surprisingly easy ways to get interviews, and you'll discover why the ideal interview is not always the one you do in person.

Focus Your Writing

Bonnie Hearn

CHAPTER FIVE

THE FOCUSED WAY TO INTERVIEW JUST ABOUT ANYONE

The secret to a great interview is you. You need to be a better listener than a talker. When you know what you're doing, a focused interview will feel easy and spontaneous to the person you are interviewing. You can do it, especially if you don't play by the rules.

No one ever taught me how to conduct an interview. I had to fake it while learning from what did and didn't work. In retrospect, I'm glad it happened that way. Through sheer ignorance, I discovered techniques that no one in his or her right mind would ever have allowed me to pursue.

Your article is only as good as your interview. If you do a sloppy and/or superficial one, the article will reflect it. Some of the greatest nonfiction writers are even better interviewers. They

Focus Your Writing

know which questions to ask and how to get the answers. So can you, if you're willing to forget everything you may have heard about interviewing and concentrate on focus.

FOUR (SURPRISINGLY EASY) WAYS TO GET AN INTERVIEW

1. The *telephone approach* is magic. Until you try it, you won't believe how easy it is. You call someone, say you're writing an article and would like to talk to Joe Blow. When Joe calls you back five minutes later, say you're writing an article for XYZ Publication, and you'd appreciate an opportunity to talk to him. If he asks if you're a staff writer, be honest.

I like the telephone approach. It's gotten me through many doors that might have otherwise been closed to me, including a few that probably should have stayed closed.

One of my closest friends is a fan of singer Eartha Kitt. When Kitt came to town for a one-woman show, my friend called and said, "I've got to meet her."

I phoned the show promoter to arrange for an interview. On the night of the show, my friend, posing as my photographer, and I arrived at the hotel where Kitt was staying. After the show, we went to Kitt's hotel room, where I conducted the interview.

We were almost caught when my friend asked, in the adoring voice of a true fan, "Do you mind if I take some pictures?"

"That's what you're here for, isn't it?" Kitt asked with her famous snarl.

It was all we could do to control our laughter. My friend snapped away, nevertheless, and I talked with Kitt about her career and how President Lyndon Johnson attempted to ruin her in the 1960s, after she publicly criticized the war in Vietnam.

Once I got over my initial feelings of intimidation, the interview was a positive one. Kitt's promoter called later to say the she loved the article, which by the way, ran without a photo. The ones my friend took were not publishable, but they make great mementos. It's still one of my favorite interviews, and it started with an innocent phone call.

2. The *letter approach* sometimes works with subjects who are more difficult to reach.

   Dear President Blow,

   I am a free-lance writer working on an article about the new tax laws. I would appreciate an opportunity to speak with you.

   I'll be phoning your secretary Monday morning and hope you'll be able to schedule me for an interview.

   Best regards,
   John Writer

3. If all else fails, you might try the *questionnaire approach*. It goes like this.

   Dear Mr. Blow,

   I am a free-lance writer researching an article on how the presidents of major corporations feel about the new tax laws.

   Enclosed is a questionnaire, which I hope you will complete and return to me by May 1.

   If you have any comments, please feel free to contact me at (209) 435-7451.

   Thank you for your time. I look forward to hearing from you.

> *Best regards,*
> *Jane Writer*

4. The final method is the *referral approach*. You know someone who knows the subject. You ask the person if she or he minds if you contact the subject. Then, using the phone or letter approach, you state, "Jane Brown suggested I contact you regarding an article I'm writing."

There you have them, the four approaches to get you through the door. Go for the phone first. I'm constantly amazed at how many famous and infamous people will accept a phone call from a writer. Even if that call doesn't get you an interview, it can get you a great quote or even a click-buzz that you can dutifully report in your finished piece.

WHAT TO ASK

Make a list of FOCUSED questions you want to ask your subject. Many of them will be for background. Others will be geared to get the subject talking. Write down the questions for reference only, but don't ask them in the order you've written them. The successful interview should be a conversation, and in order to make it so, you have to learn to LISTEN to your subject's responses.

I don't use a question sheet. Instead, I simply list the points I want covered: History of business; Turning point; Advertising philosophy; Most successful product; Greatest challenge.

WHY? is probably your most important question. HOW? is another. You can ask these questions only after your subject has answered more basic ones, so be ready to kill some time with questions that don't matter until your subject relaxes.

Bonnie Hearn
CHANGING FOCUS

You may not always know the focus of your interview until you start talking and *listening.* That's fine. The minute you smell the real story, focus your remaining questions in that direction.

An article I planned about a builder's energy-efficient home was less interesting than the builder's partnership with an interior designer. In the course of the interview, I learned that the custom subdivision in which the home was built planned a unique, cost-effective grand opening with five of the city's top restaurants serving appetizers in the subdivision's five furnished models. This resulted in a second article to a second publication.

A friend of mine wrote a holiday article dealing with the history of our city's Christmas Tree Lane. In the process of interviewing, she discovered a friendly source who told her she should talk to some of the people who live in the homes in the area and find out how they felt about being visited by hundreds of passers-by each year. While this was not the focus of her first article, my friend followed the lead and sold the second piece, "Living on the Lane," as a sidebar to the first one.

A sidebar (also known as a sidebox) is usually run in a box within or beside the main article. It gives the reader additional insight that doesn't belong in the main piece, and it earns more money for the writer. If the main article is about the popularity of food from Spain, the sidebar might be a recipe for paella. My friend's sidebar was a personal approach to a basically historical article. It worked. And it enhanced the original piece in a way it wouldn't have if the writer tried to include it in that piece. The result was focus, and for my friend, two published, paid-for articles instead of one.

How do you know when to change focus? Listen to your subject, and don't be afraid to switch your line of questioning or to come right out and tell the subject what you have in mind.

When doing an article on the original Cisco Kid, I realized that no minority actor had yet dealt with what it was like to be a Mexican hero when those parts were few. I told Duncan Renaldo so and was rewarded, once I changed focus in midstream, with many anecdotes that helped sell the final piece for more money to a better market.

BE THE SUBJECT'S NEW BEST FRIEND

A hostile subject won't give the quotes you want. Unless you're writing an exposé, assure the subject that you want him or her to look good in print. This doesn't mean you should give your subject final approval on the article. If she says, "Fax it to me," explain that while doing so is against editorial policy (yours, but don't say that), you will read back all quotes, on the phone, to check for technical accuracy.

For sensitive material you want only as background, say, "Now, this isn't for the article, but didn't you used to work for XYZ Company before the corporate takeover?"

When you're talking to a subject, your real job is to listen. Don't lead the subject.

I work with a reporter who prides herself on her knowledge of fashion. She always says something like, "We hear shorter skirts are going to be even more popular this year." Thus, her articles reflect only her own opinions, which aren't necessarily bad. She'd do better, though, if she asked the subject the most important trends and then just shut up and LISTENED. She already knows about short skirts, right? If she would give up a little control, she might learn something she doesn't know.

In order to get the subject to talk, you might need to encourage him. That's easy, and it could reward you with a good quote. Say something like, "You're pretty good at this," or "I can tell you've done this before."

At the end of the interview, you can get your best quotes. Just ask a simple question. "What else?" and shut up. You'll be amazed at what follows. You might even go as far to state your focus and say, "Is there anything I can add that will help the beginner be as successful as you are?" Or: "What can I tell the readers of this article that will make them want to rush out and buy your book?"

"REAL" VERSUS STAGED INTERVIEWS

All of this takes place during the "real" interview, which I conduct on the phone, an approach I recommend to beginners. Why? Isn't that kind of impersonal? Absolutely. As a result, the subject will be comfortable talking to you. I deal with it by telling the subject that I just need a little background information before the (staged) interview.

The subject can't see me writing madly, making faces or juggling my notes. Besides, it's "just a little background." This is when my real work is done. By the time I visit the subject, most of the article is written, and I know exactly what I need to round it out.

THE BEAUTY AND CURSE OF PRESS RELEASES

A press release can be your friend or your foe. Don't expect too much from it, and you could have a decent relationship with both it and the client it pretends to represent. Use it for basic research, such the spelling of names and the proper dates. Period. A well-written press release (which many in my business consider an oxymoron) can give you enough background to ask some intelligent questions.

In all the articles I've written, I've never used a manufactured press release quote. They almost smell contrived. When I write a press release or press kit for a client, I omit quotes, even if the client requests one or more.

The reason is simple. A good press release gives the writer enough information to conduct an in-depth interview. It never is and never can be a substitute for the real thing. These public relations pieces are strictly background, so that the subject and the writer have a starting point.

ONE LONG QUOTE

You're going to have to trust me on this one. Try writing the entire interview as one long quote while you talk to your subject (on the phone). Then you can honestly lift out whichever quote adds meat to the bones of your article.

Avoid weak quotes

> *"We sell a lot of watches," Jones said.*

So what? Paraphrase.

> *Jones said watches are his store's chief source of income.*
> *"It's the kids," he said. "They want a watch for every day of the week."*

Use only your best quotes

Go through your interview notes and highlight them, then try to work as many as you need into your article.

This is truly focus time. Never think you're obligated to use any quote that doesn't fit, not even if it's clever, and you like it.

Avoid self-serving quotes that make your article sound like an ad and your subject look pompous.

A romance novelist I once interviewed compared her marginal book, which I'll call "Virgin's Surrender," to Larry McMurtry's masterpiece, "Lonesome Dove."

"So, if you want to write another 'Lonesome Dove' or 'Virgin's Surrender,' you have to concentrate on creating real characters," she said.

I choked (but I was on the phone, remember) and asked, "Are you saying then that character is more important than plot?"

"Oh, yes. A good character actually determines the plot, and if you want to write another 'Lonesome Dove' or 'Virgin's Surrender...'"

The published quote was: *"A good character actually determines the plot,"* she said.

The article wasn't planned as a hatchet job. I did the lady a favor by saving her from her own self-serving quote, which in the long run, would not have served her well at all. She got even with me, though. The original quote turned up as sage advice in her own book on how to write fiction. The lesson here is that some subjects you interview are going to do themselves in anyway, without any help from you. When they consent to an interview, they are trusting you. Respect that trust, even if you don't respect the subject.

A SHORT WORD ABOUT TAPE RECORDERS. "DON'T"

Except as the back up it is intended to be, a tape recorder can strangle the life out of your article. I depended on one once for a medical article about the ultrasonic destruction of kidney stones. The reason, I convinced myself, was the complicated subject matter. With the recorder humming smoothly away, I talked to the doctor, settled back, enjoyed myself and forgot that I was a writer with a focus.

When I played back the tape, it was like listening to the radio. I couldn't get into the focus of the story, because I didn't feel part of it.

The same was true when I wrote my ghost winery story. I was in love with idea. I wandered through intriguing wineries asking questions, chatting with the winemakers. In the process of transcribing hour after hour of notes, I lost the magic of the piece

I had originally wanted to write. I sold the story, but I destroyed the inspiration that had led me to it.

Writing is a right-brain, creative process. You'll lose that, I truly believe, if you're involved in the left-brain process of transcribing material from a tape recorder.

The very act of taking notes makes you a part of the process and it a part of you. It involves you in a way a conversation cannot do. Besides, what happens if the recorder fails? Mine didn't, but my articles, which I managed to publish anyway, did. They were non-writing about what were then vital and fascinating subjects. I might have had every quote on tape, but I missed two rich opportunities to be more than another boring, dutiful reporter.

The focused writer doesn't need a tape recorder for anything more than the checking of facts. Write the article first, from your notes, then, when you're editing, refer to the tape for anything you might have missed or for the exact wording of quotes.

SUMMARY

The quality of the interview you conduct will determine the quality of your article. Methods of obtaining an interview include: the telephone approach, the letter approach, the questionnaire approach and the referral approach.

Make a list of questions or ideas you want to cover for background, but listen to your subject and be ready to change focus the instant you hear something more interesting than what you originally had in mind. Don't lead your subject. Listen.

Try conducting the initial phase of your interview on the telephone, telling the subject you need some background information.

Use press releases only for basic information, such as dates and spelling of names. Never use a manufactured quote.

Take notes using direct quotations, so that you can pick and choose which to include later. Avoid weak and self-serving quotes.

Use a tape recorder for back up, but don't rely on it to take notes for you. Write your article, then refer to your taped interview when you're editing. By taking notes, you'll feel part of the story, and your resulting copy will be fresher and more alive.

ASSIGNMENT

1. Get an interview with someone you think will make a good subject.

2. Resist the impulse to conduct the interview in person. Take most of your notes on the phone, using one long quote.

3. Before you as much as visit the person you interviewed, write the rough draft of your story.

4. Make a list of what you're missing. What kind of quote do you need? What vital information do you lack?

5. Now, visit the subject with your needs in mind. "Interview" to your heart's content. Get the information you need.

6. As soon as possible, plug the vital information into your rough draft.

Now you have all you need to stitch a seamless article certain to sell. The next chapter will show you how to do just that.

Focus Your Writing

Bonnie Hearn

CHAPTER SIX

STITCHING THE SEAMLESS ARTICLE

You've completed the research for an article. Scribbled pages cover your work area. Your blank-faced computer sits waiting for directions. Since your goal, at this point, is an article, not the History of the Universe, understand that you can include only the quotes and information that fit the focus of your piece.

One of the biggest mistakes beginning writers make is thinking they have to use every precious fact, every anecdote, every word from every source. They end up with a lumpy patchwork quilt instead of a seamless, flowing garment. You can't stitch a seamless piece with a scrap of this and a scrap of that. Remember the Focuscope you made from that empty toilet paper roll? Pretend you are looking at your finished article through it. What fits?

Decide first on your focus, which will determine the type of title and lead you want. You might do as Zinsser suggests and ask yourself some basic questions before you start. "In what capacity am I going to address the reader?" (Reporter? Provider of information? Average man or woman?) "What pronoun and tense am I going to use?" "What style?" (Impersonal reportorial? Personal but formal? Personal and casual?) "What attitude am I going to take toward the material?" (Involved? Detached? Judgmental? Ironic? Amused?) "How much do I want to cover?" "What one point do I really want to make?"

The last two questions are more important than they seem. "What you think is definitive today will turn undefinitive by tomorrow, and the writer who doggedly pursues every last fact will find himself pursuing the rainbow and never setting down to write," Zinsser said. "Decide what corner of your subject you are going to bite off and be content to cover it well and stop. You can always come back another day and bite off another corner."

TITLE SEARCH

I'm always a little suspicious when someone submits a manuscript to me without a title. The implication is that the writer isn't certain of the article's theme and/or intent. If the writer isn't sure, why should I invest my time trying to figure it out?

The title should be both the first and last ingredient of a focused article. The first, or working title, gives you direction. It's the title of the article you think you're going to write. You create the last after you've edited your piece. It's the title of the article you've actually written, and while it may be your working title, it doesn't have to be.

An effective title must: grab readers; convey the theme of your article; and be specific, not general. Beware of one-word, general titles such as "Love" or worse (one I've seen too many times as an editor and a writing teacher) the all-encompassing "Reflections."

A few of the title types you might consider include:

1. *The Pun*—While it has encountered a few enemies in the literary world, the pun is an effective title device if it reflects the theme of your piece. "Flame and Fortune," an article by Melissa T. Jackson, in Chile Pepper magazine, follows the title with "An exploration of art world megastar R.C. Gorman's ongoing celebration of the hot stuff, both in his art work and his kitchen."

2. *The Parody*—Like the pun, this device can be effective when it mirrors your theme. "Treasured Island," by Leslie Bennetts in Vanity Fair hooks the reader, then delivers with a longer subhead, "Eighty-one-year-old Robert Gardiner is battling fellow Social Register regular Robert Goelet for control of historic Gardiner's Island, and a few punches are being pulled."

3. *The Familiar Phrase*—Borrowing from nursery rhymes and popular culture is a way of creating reader interest, even when the original meaning is far removed from the subject of your article. "Along Came a Spider," by Suzanne Trempe, which appeared in Good Housekeeping, tells the story of Cindy Winegar, who after being bitten by an "innocent-looking brown insect," almost lost her arm.

4. *The Rhyme*—Before you try this one, consider the subject of the piece and your target publication. If it's Cosmopolitan, for instance, you might concoct a title like Roberta Israeloff's "Are you a crybaby? Here's why, baby."

5. *The Alliterative*—If you come on like Edgar Allan Poe, your attempts at alliteration can jar the reader right out of the mood you're attempting to create. Try something subtle, such as, "Seven Great Moves to Boost Your Behind" by Eric Sternlict, Ph.D. and George Salem, Ph.D., which promises the readers of Shape just that.

6. ***The Unexpected***—"Dancing with God," by Ann McMath in Guideposts, compares a ballroom dancing class with scripture. It's an unusual title, reflecting an even more unusual theme, and it works.

BEGIN AT THE BEGINNING?

Contrary to what you might have heard, you do not begin an article at the beginning. You don't begin a fiction piece there either, but that's another story for another book.

Until you master the craft, use highlighter pens to mark good quotes and good information from your volumes of interviews and research. The first rule is to write, right now, while the interview is fresh. The longer you wait, the more stale it will become.

BILLBOARD STATEMENT

Whether you think of it as the Billboard Statement, Establishment Paragraph, Statement of Theme, Nutgraph, or any of the other clever names it is called, you must, at some point, tell your reader what he is going to learn as a result of reading your article.

Coffee lovers have been known to go to great lengths to find the best beans and keep them fresh. Now for about half the price of top-quality coffee beans and with only an electric popcorn popper, you can roast your own beans at home.

The first sentence is a Theme Lead. The second is a Billboard Statement. If this were your article, you might want to make a new paragraph and use a quote from a coffee expert.

Bonnie Hearn
SELECTING AND VARYING QUOTES

You already have picked out, maybe highlighted, the best quotes from your interview. You know to avoid self-serving quotes and ordinary quotes that could be just as easily paraphrased. The statements that stand out, reveal something and really sparkle are the ones you want to incorporate in your article.

You can vary quotes by breaking them up or paraphrasing them.

Break Up a Long Quote

"More and more people are wanting to roast their own beans these days," said Joe Blow, president of United Coffee Roasters Inc. "People like the fact that, coffee beans, until they're roasted, actually improve with age."

Or Paraphrase the Quote

Roasting coffee beans at home is increasing in popularity, said Joe Blow, president of United Coffee Roasters Inc.

"People like the fact, that coffee beans, until they're roasted, actually improve with age."

Although fiction writers know to separate quotes by paragraphs each time a new character speaks, some disagreement exists about where quotes should be broken in an article. While an editor may change it later, you'll be safer if you let the quotes stand alone in their own paragraphs as in the above example, where the paraphrase is one paragraph and the quote another. That way there'll be no confusion as to which is your opinion and which is Joe Blow's.

An exception to this rule is when you're quoting a word or phrase. Employ this device when you need to vary quotes or when most of what Joe Blow said was pretty dull. You can also use it when you're paraphrasing and you want to make it clear that the word or words are Joe Blow's and not yours.

According to Joe Blow, president of United Coffee Roasters Inc., an increasing number of "coffee nuts" are roasting their beans at home.

"They're using everything from electric skillets to hot-air popcorn poppers," Blow said. "Our sales of green coffee beans have tripled in less than two years."

Paraphrase part or all of the quote when it would require rewriting to work.

Don't ever manufacture a quote and don't ever, ever use a quote someone else, even if it's the subject, manufactured. Nothing will destroy your credibility faster.

"JOE" OR "MR. BLOW"?

The Associated Press Stylebook says to refer to your source by last name after you have identified him. Study the publication for which you are writing and handle quotes accordingly. For a Family Circle article, I referred to the subject as Marilyn, her first name, throughout the piece. For a newspaper article about the same woman, I referred to her, after the first reference, as Hamilton, her last name. For AP articles, he's Joe Blow in the first reference and Blow for subsequent references.

JOE BLOW ENTHUSED? LET'S HOPE NOT

Use said. It's a wonderful word, and it tends to be invisible, so that the reader doesn't pause or stumble over it. Joe Blow said. Not says, not added, not explained, not reflected, not ejaculated, not commented and certainly not continued. All these terms will make you sound like a public-relations writer, the kiss of death.

ATTRIBUTION

Don't say: *The process of roasting your own beans will produce a rich, delicious coffee that is superior to anything you'll find in a restaurant.*

That sounds as if it's your opinion. If it's Joe Blow's opinion, attribute it to him. The exception is a review or a personal-experience article, where your opinion is the focus.

MULTI-SOURCE ARTICLES

Suppose you're quoting not only Joe Blow but Jane Jones, editor of a coffee-lovers' catalog? You can still start with Blow's quotes, as we have above. When you're ready for Jones' quote, just introduce her and proceed as you did with Blow.

> *Home roasters are now available at reasonable prices, said Jane Jones, editor of Java Jive magazine.*
> *"One company manufactures a roaster that retails for under $50," she said. "It will produce an espresso roast in about 30 minutes."*

In subsequent references (if you're using AP style), refer to Blow and Jones by their last names. If you're quoting Joe Blow and his wife Jane Blow, continue using their first and last names (Joe Blow said. Jane Blow said.) throughout the piece.

CONNECTING YOUR FACTS

Writing the article involves connecting quotes and facts you've gained through research into a smooth, finished piece that flows. When you're focused, you know which information belongs in this article and which should go in a sidebar, your idea file or the garbage can.

Facts can be woven in with transitional phrases, such as: *Five of California's leading coffee experts said the home-roasting craze is a result of the public's increased interest in gourmet and flavored coffees. Or: Two of the most popular beans are from Guatemala and Jamaica.*

You can also use bullets to connect facts. If your computer won't cooperate, use the * mark. In our coffee article, we could bullet each type of bean and then write a short descriptive paragraph.

If you prefer, you can forget the bullet and list the type of bean in italics or bold print. Use whatever best incorporates your information and quotations into the article.

Again. Don't think you have to use every bit of information or every quote. Your goal is to write a focused article. Toss everything that doesn't naturally fit.

SUMMARY

In order to write a seamless article, you must include only that information that fits the focus of your piece.

An effective title will both hook the reader and convey the theme of your article. Specific titles work better than general ones. Consider the pun, the parody, the familiar phrase, the rhyme, the alliterative and the unexpected.

Your article should include a Billboard Statement, so that the reader understands the purpose of the piece.

Break up long quotes or paraphrase quotes. Stick with "said" and avoid public relations dialogue tags, such as "enthused." Attribute statements of opinion to the subject, so that it is clear that they may not be your opinions.

To make one segment of the article flow naturally to the next, connect facts and quotes with transitional phrases and/or bullets.

ASSIGNMENT

1. Just one assignment this time, a big one. Incorporate your title, quotes and facts into a rough draft. Experiment with leads and choose the one that works for this article.

In creating a rough draft, you may already write the natural conclusion to your piece. Like many, you may find that knowing where to stop is as difficult as knowing where to start. The next chapter will show you how to create a short, focused finale.

Focus Your Writing

Bonnie Hearn

CHAPTER SEVEN

THE LAST WORD, OR HOW TO FINISH WITH A BANG

Although I've worked as an editor since 1982, I'm still amazed at how few writers know how to effectively conclude an article. Without the right conclusion, a potentially good piece can lose its focus, leave the reader unfulfilled and trail off into generalities.

The conclusion of an article has its own purpose, just as the lead does. If you've read this far, you already know that the lead is the promise, the body is the proof, and the conclusion is the payoff. Promise, Proof and Payoff create a focused article.

Your last paragraph, especially your last sentence, should achieve two important goals. First, it must satisfy your reader, who's been hanging in there for 2,000-plus-or-minus words, following you dutifully from point to point, wondering how it will end. Second, it must reflect your theme. Ideally, you should accomplish both of these goals without coming across as self-conscious or heavy-handed.

Many writers feel a need to refer back to the lead in an article's conclusion. As a rule, it's best to avoid this device. Referring back to your lead is almost like a big "The End" at the conclusion of your article. You don't have to be that obvious.

Others try to conclude with punctuation marks instead of words. Don't make the mistake of trying to use exclamation points or ellipses as crutches to hold up a weak piece.

In my experience, the following ending types work best.

THE RELEVANT QUOTE

This is one of the most common methods of concluding an article, and it's still often a good one.

A quote is real and alive. It's not a literary hammer the writer manufactures to drive home a specific point. It's something that somebody related to the issue really said, and so has built-in validity.

A relevant quote will work in almost every type of article, from personal-opinion pieces to news stories.

Sometimes a quote from a subject you haven't even mentioned in the article works best. Joan Ullman used one in "I carried it too far, that's for sure," a first-person report from the Jeffrey Dahmer insanity trial, that appeared in Psychology Today.

Ullman begins her article with a Shocking-Statement Lead.

> *Milwaukee—famed for its beer, cheese, chocolate and sausages—has a Summerfest and a Winterfest. For three weeks last month I was astonished to find that this predominantly German "great city on a great lake" also had a "Dahmerfest."*

After describing the hideous aspects of the trial, she makes a powerful Billboard Statement.

> *I became convinced that the insanity defense is an insanity that should be scrapped.*

Ullman follows that with numerous quotes that support the theme, then ends with:

> *The first really sane talk I heard after all this came from the cab driver who drove me to the airport after the verdict was announced. "Those psychiatrists talk a lot, but they don't know what they are talking about," he said. "They can't agree on anything. First they should define sanity."*

THE RELATED FACT

By its very brevity, a related fact can bring home your theme in an unexpected way, supporting the writer's opinion without blatantly stating it.

This type of ending can add an element of surprise when you're writing about an emotional topic, especially one that's been overworked by the press. It's also a handy substitute for the relevant quote when you don't have a quote powerful enough to finish with.

In "Battered Wives, Shattered Lives," which appeared in Family Circle, Edward Tivnan starts the story with a Case History Lead.

> *Mollie had never called the police before—not even during her first pregnancy when he got so mad he hurled a dart into her back. Or the time he gave her a black eye in the middle of the airport.*

The proof of the article is comprised of quotes from Mollie and women like her, as well as law-enforcement officials and representatives of battered women's groups. Tivnan presents his four most riveting statistics by setting them off with bullets and a short, powerful introduction: *The statistics hit you—well, like a slap in the face.*

He ends by returning to the subject of his lead, then concludes with this.

> *But tragically—and any story about domestic violence, no matter how hopeful, remains tragic—most victims of battering have nowhere to go. In the entire country there are only 1,500 shelters for battered women and children. There are 3,807 animal shelters.*

The animal shelter fact could have been placed anywhere in the story. By putting it at the end, the author delivers a bitter punch line (payoff) to an already emotionally charged piece.

THE LAST DETAIL

When you're writing a straightforward article with a clear, informational purpose—"Ten Ways to Beat the Summer Blues," "Twelve Safety Rules for Winter Driving"—don't try too hard to concoct a clever finish. The payoff is the final point. When the list ends, the article ends as well.

If you're writing a list article such as, "The Dirty Dozen," about common scams that snag even smart women, which Arnold Diaz published in Redbook, you can simply finish with your last item.

Diaz begins with a Theme Lead.

> *Not all robbers carry guns or knives. Some use wiles to cheat you out of money; they sell you phony merchandise and promise*

opportunities that are too good to be true. Many of these schemes are aimed at women.

Diaz divides the article into 12 sections, "the dirty dozen." Under each heading, he then describes one scam, and then follows with a short paragraph of advice.

His 12th and final entry is the end of the article. The piece has accomplished what it set out to do, and the payoff is complete.

THE JOKE

If the tone of your article is light, a humorous ending might work for you.

In his Writer's Digest article, "Elvis Reveals: Writers Make Millions Selling to Tabloids!," Donald Vaughan sets up his tone right from the title (complete with tabloid-style exclamation point). Headings are written as tabloid headlines such as "Writer Unearths Mutant Article Idea!" and "Writer's Manuscripts Circle the Earth."

His Direct Address Lead goes like this:

> *You can't push a cart through a supermarket checkout without being assaulted by racks of them. They scream at you with outrageous stories about Elizabeth Taylor, Magic Johnson, Bigfoot and cyclops babies. Every heading is a Hey Martha! designed to make you plunk down your hard-earned 95 cents for the latest dirt on Hollywood or the newest super-diet. Tabloid newspapers are big business, and there's plenty of room for you to be a part of it.*

Focus Your Writing

The entertaining style fits the theme of Vaughan's piece, which incidentally, contains solid tips. His conclusion makes its point, then leaves the reader with a smile.

> *I could talk about the tabloids all day, but you'll have to excuse me now. I'm having Elvis over for dinner, and then we're going for a ride in his UFO.*
>
> *I might even get a story out of it.*

THE ANECDOTE

Leaving your reader with a story instead of a sermon can really make personal-experience and personal-opinion articles strike home.

For it to work, the anecdote should be short and pertinent to your theme. A good story isn't good enough.

Many inspirational writers use anecdotal conclusions. Hugh Herr did in "Scaling the Heights," which he wrote for Guideposts.

Herr, a rock climber, lost both legs below the knees after being trapped in a blizzard when he was 16.

He started his first-person story like this:

> *When I first looked down at the hospital sheet, flat below my knees, I cried out in agony. I knew gangrene in my legs had necessitated the amputations. But they had cut off so much! Could I ever climb again?*

The article deals with Herr's search for artificial limbs. He majors in physics. He begins working with a certified artificial-limb specialist. He prays. In the course of the story, he meets 16-year-old Giles Thompson, who has just lost his lower legs in a blizzard. He remembers the scripture, "Blessed are those who have not seen and yet believe" (John 20:29).

Herr writes:

> *I prayed for Giles and couldn't get him out of my mind. Now more than ever, I knew I had to press on in our search for a comfortable prosthetic socket, not just for me, but for all the Giles Thompsons in the world.*
>
> *...as with those who have seen and yet believe, I know that when we strive for the sake of others, and when we believe, we can accomplish.*

The article could have ended there. Instead, Herr concludes with an anecdote that makes his success even more satisfying to the reader:

> *Not long ago, I went to Oregon to confer with a prosthetist. As we talked in his office, in through the door walked a confident-looking young man. When he saw me, his bright blue eyes lit up, and he strode forward, hand outstretched. It was Giles Thompson, who will be one of the first to wear our new fluid prosthetic socket.*

THE EDITORIAL

To work, an editorial conclusion must be short; sometimes even a word or two will suffice. It's most effective when the writer's opinion is as important as the subject of the piece, and it also works well in first-person, personal-experience articles. Be careful with it, though. Often your opinion can be conveyed in a more subtle manner.

Maureen Orth uses the editorial ending effectively in her Vanity Fair profile "Proud Mary," about Mary Robinson, the first woman president of Ireland.

Orth begins by setting this scene:

> *She is walking alone behind the gnarled men of the village who have come to greet her with a big green satin banner that says, "May God Save Ireland." She considers herself in the same business these days. Along the way the schoolchildren have lined up on both sides of the road, and the junior band, all apple-cheeked and scrubbed for the biggest day this tiny place has seen in perhaps centuries, is playing tin whistles in a rousing Presidential Salute. It is a tableau of tradition and timelessness in the Irish countryside except that it has never happened before and would not have but for her.*

She finishes the article with a quote from philosopher Richard Kearney, and then a short editorial statement of only two words.

> *"With Mary Robinson," says Kearney, "we're into a revision and a whole reimagining of Ireland as a sister, as a modern woman." Hail Mary.*

THE IMPERATIVE

The imperative instructs the reader to *do* something, and can add power and a sense of urgency to an article. It works best in how-to articles and some editorials and reviews, in which you're expected to offer an opinion or give some kind of advice ("Try this restaurant," "Don't miss this film," "Vote yes on Issue 2").

I chose an imperative to end this chapter because I felt it best demonstrates my final point. See if you agree:

> *The more focused articles you write, the easier it will be to recognize the best way to end them. You might even begin to think of possible endings midway through your first draft. Until you reach that stage, see if one of these ending types might work for a story you're having trouble wrapping up. And remember that you don't have to wave your ending under your reader's nose. Just stop.*

SUMMARY

The conclusion of an article is the payoff. It must both satisfy your reader and reflect your theme. Avoid just repeating the lead or resorting to excessive punctuation marks.

Types of endings that work include: the relevant quote, the related fact, the last detail, the joke, the anecdote, the editorial and the imperative.

When you've found your conclusion, stop writing. Don't belabor the point.

ASSIGNMENT

1. Examine several articles in the publication to which you'd like to submit. Highlight the leads and conclusions. Try to identify the types of conclusions the authors used. Would a different conclusion have worked better?

2. Go over the first draft of your article. Is your conclusion subtle, focused and relevant to your theme? Avoid repeating or restating the lead or the title of the piece.

Focus Your Writing

3. Ask yourself what type of article you're writing. Is it a straightforward piece that doesn't require a dramatic finale? A personal-opinion piece or essay that begs for a one-on-one imperative or editorial finish?

4. Read your first draft, even your notes. Underline any related fact or relevant quote that might work better as an ending than in the body of your text.

5. Make a check mark by any good anecdotes that might echo your theme in a conclusion. Is the anecdote connected to something you've already mentioned in the story? Does it feel as if it's part of the story, not something you tacked on to make your point?

6. Finally, read your article aloud to yourself. Does the piece flow to the conclusion. Are you satisfied as a *reader* when you reach the end?

In the last chapters, you've learned the basics of constructing a marketable article. You've been in a creating mode, writing with little regard for anything but getting your story down. Now it's time to switch gears from writer to editor.

CHAPTER EIGHT

FOCUSED EDITING: THE LAST STEP BEFORE YOU SUBMIT

Editors are made, not born. Many gifted writers never publish because they fail to develop their editing skills. They drift from first draft to first draft, avoid rewrites and never enjoy the success that comes only to finishers.

Editing gives you a sense of power. You are able to send your story into the world feeling confident that it is the best you can possibly make it.

But won't a *real* editor do all that later? Not any more when many of us receive hundreds of manuscripts a day. An editor will correct style, but first, your manuscript has to be focused enough to warrant our attention.

Your editing lacks focus when you read your piece as the writer, correcting spelling and punctuation, but not really determining if it works as a whole. *Focused* editing is cutting away everything, regardless of how good it is or how dear it is to

Focus Your Writing

you, that doesn't contribute to the theme and pace of the manuscript.

FOCUSED EDITING

It takes time at first, but it can make the difference between a sale and a rejection.

- Circle, then kill unnecessary adjectives and adverbs
- Circle, then exchange passive verbs for power verbs
- Eliminate redundancies and unnecessary paragraphs, especially at the beginning and end of the article
- Define punctuation. Omit exclamation points, ellipses, etc., most colons and semi-colons and orphan quotes
- Keep your style consistent with a style book or the style of the publication

Focus Your Writing

You must forget that this is your baby and approach your task with total ruthlessness. The purpose of focused editing is to find what's wrong, not marvel over what's right. In order to accomplish that, you need some distance.

Archibald MacLeish said he liked to put his poems in a drawer, like apples, so that they had a chance to either ripen or well, you know what can happen to apples in a drawer. His point is that you are better able to observe what's ripe and what's rotten when you step back from your creation for a time.

Don't try to edit while you write. Nothing should hold you back while you're in the creative mode. When you've finished your first draft (which some call a discovery draft), let the poor thing rest a little, then return to it with the objective, analytical eyes of an editor.

LISTEN TO YOURSELF

Read the manuscript aloud. Slowly. Make a check mark whenever it appears to bog down or fail to focus.

Now, read it again. Are you getting really sick of it? Good. Your diminishing infatuation will help you find additional areas to check.

The essence of focus is telling your story without making the reader aware of the writer. That reader wants to **experience** the story, not marvel at your wonderful prose. Remember William Faulkner's advice and "kill your darlings." Underline the line or phrase you love most, then seriously consider killing it.

We don't usually love a line because it contributes to the overall story but because it fills an emotional need or makes us feel brilliant. At the editing stage, what you feel about yourself doesn't matter. Kill that darling before it kills your piece.

Bonnie Hearn

REWORK PASSIVE CONSTRUCTIONS

Your tools are strong nouns, power verbs and a minimum of adjectives and adverbs. Check your verbs. Are they too passive? Do you use *was, were, is*, when you could use more powerful verbs? Would *sold* be better than *is selling*? Could *There was an increase in sales* be changed to *An increase in sales resulted in...?*

A man was walking into the room. Pretty pale and passive, isn't it? What about *A man walked into the room.* Or better, *A man sauntered into the room. A man, strolled, marched, stumbled into the room.*

This is what is meant by the admonition, "Show, don't tell." By your choice of verbs, you can show the reader a great deal about the attitude and personality of the man entering the room.

A sunset could be seen in the distance. More passivity. Seen by whom? Try using the sunset as the subject and coming up with a power verb such as *blazed, dwindled, faded.*

KILL EXCESSIVE ADJECTIVES AND ADVERBS

Go through and circle all adjectives and adverbs. How many do you need? Avoid that nasty little habit of shoving two adjectives together.

"It was a dark and stormy night" became a literary joke for a reason. One adjective is weak. Two, especially when they attempt to prop up each other, are as ineffective as two drunks staggering down a sidewalk.

This is another time to remember, "Show, don't tell." If someone is angry, you can show that by what she says, not by writing something like, *"Get out of here, you jerk," she said angrily.*

PICK UP THE PACE

In fiction, pace is action. If many events take place, the pace is fast. If the main character squats on a camp stool in front of his apartment building and contemplates the meaning of life, the pace is slow, not to mention deadly.

A screenwriter I know compares writing to attending a cocktail party. "You need to come late and leave early," he says. This is sound advice, whether you're writing a poem, a short story, a novel or an essay.

An article needs to move right along. You want fact, fact, fact. Quote, quote, quote. Beginning, middle, end. Promise, proof, payoff. If your article is too slow, ask yourself how much you can take away and still make your point.

With a blank piece of paper, cover your first paragraph. Will the article still work without it? If so, cover your second paragraph. Continue this test until you find the true beginning of your story.

Move to the end of the article and cover up the last paragraph. Will the article work without it? What about the next-to-the-last paragraph? Be brutal.

Length is not the same as pace. A story can be 2,000 words and still be the **wrong** 2,000 words.

As we've just discussed, ridding your manuscript of passive verbs, especially *is, was* and other forms of *to be* is the fastest way to improve its pace. Eliminating redundancy is another. If you use a word or phrase, don't repeat it right away.

A slow pace can also result from too many and/but compound sentences, or worse, too many sentences starting with *and* or *but*. "But I'm just trying to sound informal," you say. "And I don't see why I can't write this way. So I just think I'll continue to do so. And I don't care what you think."

I see too many potentially good manuscripts that are flawed in this way. And/but are connectors. Too many make your whole piece read like one, long run-on sentence.

PARE DOWN PUNCTUATION

Punctuation exists to clarify and make the process of reading as effortless as possible. Learn grammar and punctuation if you have to enroll in a correspondence course or invest a few evenings of your life at the local adult school.

Regardless of how much you love water, you wouldn't jump into the ocean without knowing how to swim. The literary world is the ultimate ocean, and you'll drown in one swift second if you believe anyone will attempt to look past your lack of skill and see the natural talent beneath.

Go through your article and ask yourself if you've capitalized the words that should be and not fallen into the cap-trap that snares most public relations writers. The trend today is downstyle, that is, minimal capitalization. *His mother. Her mom. I talked to Mom about it.* Be careful of words like the Home Buyer and the Loan Department that should not be capitalized.

If you're writing anything other than a scholarly article, kill most semi-colons, colons and exclamation marks residing there. The semi-colon and its cousin, the colon, seldom belong in consumer magazines and never in quotes. They make the reader aware that a writer is flailing in there somewhere, and they lend a too-scholarly tone to the most reader-friendly pieces.

Exclamation points and ellipses are enemies of the beginning writers. We use such tools because... well, because... we somehow sense the writing is weak... and we hope these tools... the exclamation point, the ellipsis... sometimes a word or a sentence in capital letters... will strengthen it and make it POWERFUL!!!! It doesn't work. Does it?

Don't use ellipses in place of a dash or a period. Refrain from capital letters to make your point. Remember that F. Scott Fitzgerald said using an exclamation point is like laughing at your own joke.

He didn't say laughing at your own joke, etc. Avoid this horrible habit. Etc. is a crutch for writers who don't know what they want to say.

Focus Your Writing

If cats, dogs and a few rare birds occupied the pet shop, say so. Ask yourself what you mean by etc. and substitute solid language.

AVOID ORPHAN QUOTES

An orphan quote is a word or phrase, enclosed in quotation marks, that isn't attributed to anyone. It goes something like this:

> *The "chubby" woman insisted that heavy people are healthier. Her "snack" that day consisted of two hot-fudge sundaes.*

Or:

> *The big "thrill" in those "happy days" was driving our old "clunker" down "Main."*

Orphan quotes belong to no one. The writer simply decides to use them to show that the word or phrase isn't very original. These quotes are like underlining. By trying to make a point, they draw attention to weak writing. Send them back to the orphanage and come up with a fresh word or phrase you won't have to qualify with excessive punctuation.

AVOID USAGE PITFALLS

It is difficult for an editor to turn away from a writer who demonstrates respect for and a command of the language. That's not to say that proper usage alone will get you published. Ridding your manuscript of these common errors, however, will give your work a polished, more professional look.

Bonnie Hearn

1. ***Advance warning.*** As is the case with advance planning, omit the *advance.* What other kind is there?

2. ***Beautiful.*** Robert Frost said, when he was in his 80s, that a poet could use the word beautiful just three times in his life. "And I still have two times coming," Frost said. Try comparisons instead of superlatives. Instead of *She was the most beautiful woman in the world* (a superlative), consider, *She was more beautiful than his wife.* Or *She was so beautiful, that even hard-bitten Jones, the gardener, stepped aside and smiled as she passed.*

3. ***Enthused.*** If the person is enthusiastic, say so. Not: *"I'm going to the ball," Cinderella enthused.*

4. ***Its'.*** Never use an apostrophe to indicate the possessive form of it. The only time you use *it's* is when it's a contraction of it is. *It's an elegant hotel, right down to the antique furniture in its rooms.*

5. ***Reoccur.*** The word is recur.

6. ***Firstly, secondly, lastly.*** First, he went to class. Second, he handed in his work.

7. ***Preventative.*** Yes, there is such a word. It is a noun, however. Vitamin C is a preventative. Taking it to avoid getting a cold is a preventive measure. Preventive modifies measure.

8. ***First annual.*** There's no such thing as a first annual event, only a second annual and any number beyond that.

9. ***Myriad of.*** Myriad, which means a vast number, comes from the Greek word for 10,000. It's overused by myriad writers,

who use it, often incorrectly, as an attempt to class up their work.

10. ***1990s** or any other year followed by an apostrophe*. If you say the '90s or the '60s, you need an apostrophe to show that you mean the 1990s or the 1960s. If you learned your ABCs, you need no apostrophe to indicate the fact. The only time you do is if you're dealing with a single letter such as in the sentence, *I got all A's in school.*

An exception is when you use a possessive, such as *Today's retailers are promoting what is nothing more than a reincarnation of '60's fashions.* You could make the sentence easier to read by changing *'60's*, the possessive, to *1960's,* still a possessive, or by altering your sentence to read, *the fashions of the '60s.*

DEVELOPING STYLE

Does all this sound like an attempt to snuff out your creativity? Believe it or not, you'll be more creative when you edit your piece according to style.

"But I'm developing my own style, my own voice," you say.

That's great, Virginia, and it's time you learned that two types of style—theirs and yours—coexist in the world of writing. The first is the style a given publication has selected in order to keep its articles and stories consistent.

Every publication has a style. Most newspapers use the Associated Press Stylebook. It's like the answer book you always wished you could snitch when your high school English teacher left the room during a test. At one glance, you can see that correct AP Style is *10 percent*, not ten %. You know that John Jones, Jr. should be quoted as *John Jones Jr.* (regardless of what he may have on his business card) and that Jones, Incorporated is, for your purpose, at least, *Jones Inc.* No comma.

If you don't have a Stylebook or sheet, read your target publication and follow the rules of that style.

The second style is you. The way you write. It's what makes your article on rodeo clowns different than Mary Jane's or Hunter Thompson's. Lucky for you, no amount of thinking about the style you want will help you develop it. Only writing and focusing on your writing message will teach you to strip away enough words to discover the person and the style beneath them.

"Don't worry about your personal writing style," Gary Provost said. "It's not something that Tom Wolfe has and you lack; it's just that his is more distinctive. In time you will fall into writing patterns, you'll develop a habit of doing it this way more often than that way. You don't have to consciously cultivate a style. Just learn to write well, and your style will emerge.... Remember that your primary goal as a writer is not to leave your imprint on the page. Your goal is to *make the writing work,* make it do what it is supposed to do, cause laughter, tears, fright, anger, curiosity...."

Creativity loves a good challenge. You can't kill it. When you're a ruthless editor, when you avoid easy writing, your style will take care of itself.

"Style is organic to the person doing the writing, as much a part of him as his hair, or, if he is bald, his lack of it," William Zinsser said. "Trying to add style is like adding a toupee."

Don't be afraid to edit yourself, to throw away that metaphorical toupee and shave your prose down to the scalp. The result will be a focused manuscript that looks absolutely effortless

SUMMARY

Focused editing will enable you to submit a polished, professional piece. Never attempt to edit while you write. Start by stepping back from your manuscript and putting it away for a time.

Once you've achieved editorial distance, read the manuscript aloud and check the places where it slows down.

Kill the phrases you love most, your "darlings."

Rewrite was/were constructions. Omit excessive adjectives and adverbs, exclamation points, ellipses and orphan quotes.

Control pace by starting and finishing as close to your real story as possible. Eliminate redundancies and too many and/but sentences.

Follow the style of your target publication, and don't attempt to insert a personal style.

ASSIGNMENT

This chapter and the process of self-editing is your assignment. When you complete it, you'll have a focused article that is ready to sell.

One marketing ploy too few writers consider is winning writing contests. Notice that I didn't say *entering* writing contests.

If you want to *win,* you have to know why most entries don't make it, as well as how to tailor your entry for the judges. You'll be able to do that after reading the next chapter.

CHAPTER NINE

THE FOCUSED WAY TO WIN

Winning a writing contest can earn your work the attention it deserves. Your prize may be anything from $100 and a box of Florida oranges (Florida State University) to a trip to Italy (the Hemingway competition) or even $10,000 (The Heekin Fellowship).

Most contests request unpublished manuscripts. You can often submit the work for publication after it's been entered.

Another reason to investigate contests is the discipline imposed by a real deadline. You may find yourself speeding downtown to the post office at midnight, but when you watch that envelope slide into the mail slot, you'll step back with a rush of pride. You've finished something, anything. You have a manuscript *out there,* a piece that, win or lose, you might be able to sell.

CONTEST SOURCES

As you study the markets, you'll learn where to locate the best contests for you. Writer's Digest magazine lists many each month. The good ones usually appear as editorial information, not paid-for ads.

Writer's Digest holds its own monthly contest, which awards free books, and an annual contest with the top prize of a trip to New York. The National Writers Association newsletter, Writing For Money and Poets & Writers magazine are excellent contest sources.

As you study these markets, consider credibility, not just the cash amount of the prize. Amelia magazine paid $200 to a friend of mine who won the magazine's erotic fiction contest. Still, Amelia is far more prestigious than those buy-a-book poetry "anthologies" that award thousands but rip off many beginning writers in the process.

A JUDGE'S PERSPECTIVE

When I began entering contests, I would have given anything to know what the judges knew. Years later, when I began judging contests, I discovered those secrets:

1. *The manuscript with the most potential seldom wins.* The most *complete* manuscript does.

Potential is a scary little animal. It smiles. It darts here and there, peeking out from behind a pile of prose just when you're about to give up on it. A sincere judge keeps on reading, hoping against hope, that this talented writer will get it together by the next paragraph, the next page.

It never happens, and the judge finally turns away from even the most engaging potential.

Rewrite. Read your manuscript aloud and rewrite again. Judges have checklists. Your manuscript will be rated on a number of qualities it had better possess if it's going to make the finals.

I've often been intrigued by a writer's idea, characters or prose, but had to disqualify the manuscript because it fell down in terms of pace, point-of-view or technique.

Again, the story or article that wins is *complete*. While it may not be brilliant, it has enough of the right ingredients to stand on its own against those by writers of possibly greater talent.

2. *It's the simple stuff that gets you thrown out of the running.*

You labor over your darling for months. You polish your prose to Tiffany perfection. You rewrite again and again. Then, you send that baby off, past deadline, twice as long as the rules dictate, without that final spell-check.

I'm not exaggerating. This is what you do. This is what I do. We are so in love with our creation that we convince ourselves a judge will see through those boring technical requirements to the brilliance at its core.

Judges can only evaluate what they receive. They're looking for finished, focused products. Your botched-up baby, wonderful as it is, will be tossed if it violates even one of the contest rules.

3. *Most of what is entered just isn't that good.* I never realized how many really horrible manuscripts are entered in contests.

I've encountered short stories without a single scene or line of dialogue. I've read numerous moon-June poems that can't even follow their own simplistic meters. I've seen articles so self-serving and self-obsessed that they had to come straight from the writer's journal.

While the emotion that inspired these pieces was probably genuine, the work itself is so poor that I feel I'm watching a third-rate juggler dropping his rubber balls at the local carnival.

Focus Your Writing

A judge can sense a winner by the first or second paragraph. Your voice, your sense of story, must be there from the first word you put down.

Sandy Whelchel, director of National Writers Association, shared with me three reasons manuscripts failed in NWA's short story contest.

They had no hook. The story started too far back in the past, instead of in the middle of things.

The stories were told instead of shown. Great stories, but no active scenes. If this is your problem, I recommend any of Jack Bickham's books (Writer's Digest has several in print). You can't write a story without a scene, and Bickham is a master.

Okay. Close your eyes. Try to guess the final reason these manuscripts failed. No, don't peek. Take a wild guess.

Did you guess *technical problems?* You're right. Some manuscripts were too long, others too short, and too many writers submitted third carbon copies with strikeover corrections, Whelchel said.

There's no excuse for that. Most of us have computers with spell-check systems these days. The errors Whelchel encounters we can control. Fix them, and your manuscript will come that much closer to being a winner.

LEARNING FROM THE WINNERS

Much of what you need to know about how to win a contest can be learned from past entries. Send for copies of former winners (most are available for an SASE), and you will see what the judging sheet encompasses. You don't have to like the winning entry. Instead of bemoaning its weaknesses, ask yourself why this piece worked for one or a number of judges. How is it complete in a way your own entry may not be?

Bonnie Hearn

THE CONTEST WINNER'S CHECKLIST

Title

Whether you choose to enter something you've already written or something you're writing for this contest, pay close attention to the title of your piece. If it reflects the theme, you have a better chance of winning.

Go through and highlight every word, phrase or line that conveys your theme. Pay attention to the last line, which, even if it is subtle and understated, should be the best line in the piece. If you carefully study these words, phrases and lines, *in terms of what you think you're trying to say*, you'll be on your way to a title that reflects the theme without blaring that theme like a neon sign.

Subject matter

This is also an important consideration. Certain themes fare well in contests.

If the focus of the entry is too small, something only an esoteric group can understand, your luck will have to work overtime. Universal themes stand the best chance.

This doesn't mean that just any old poem on love, life or death will win unless it approaches the subject with a different focus.

Emotional appeal

One of my students won a major contest with a poem about her Russian grandmother. When we talked about her victory, my student reminded me of something I had said in class when we discussed the first draft of her poem: *"Kick them in the stomach and run."*

In other words, if you're dealing with an emotional subject, get in, make your point, then get out while the reader is at the height of involvement.

Playing by the rules

When you receive your contest guidelines, go through and highlight the rules, starting with the contest deadline. Most people submit on (or after) the deadline. The judges just might have more time with your work if you send it early.

You must also pay attention to word count. If it's 250 words, don't make your margins narrower so that you can send 500 words on a single page. If you're required to remove your name from your entry, don't just mail off your most recent reject or as some writers in one contest I judged cut off the upper corner of the page that contains your name.

Subject matter is also important. If the guidelines specify on what qualities the manuscript will be judged, highlight these and try to honestly rate your entry. If it's a romance novel contest, your entry had better read like a romance, not a science-fiction novel.

Most contests have rating systems for evaluating manuscripts. If yours doesn't fit, it's tossed out even by the most considerate judges. Take it from someone who's been there. Don't waste your postage or your time.

Each type of contest has its own rules, and once you learn to play by them, those rules will be second nature to you.

PRIZE-WINNING POEMS

Poetry contests award prizes for books of poems, chapbooks and individual poems.

Books of poems usually have to be at least 48 pages. If some of the poems have already appeared in literary magazines, you'll have a better chance of winning.

Send your best poems and come up with a great title that gives a theme to the piece. Include, if the rules permit it, a sheet with titles of poems and publications in which they have appeared and/or awards they have won.

Timely sources for these contests are Poets & Writers magazine and Writers Market.

A chapbook contest gives a beginning poet or a poet who is between books a chance to publish as few as 10 poems and receive a cash award.

Prior publication is still important, but not as much so in a chapbook contest. If you have credits, and if the rules allow it, include a credits page.

The best source for chapbook contests is Poets & Writers magazine.

Individual poems can be entered into any number of contests. You'll have a better chance if you study the publication for which they are intended. If it is a general, *legitimate* contest, such as the Writer's Digest annual competition, send for the printout of the previous year's winners. See what has appealed to past judges. How does your poem rate in comparison?

You need to read publications for writers and maybe even join poetry groups. Then, pick your very best poem, the one that speaks to the most people in the most original way.

AWARD-WINNING ARTICLES

If you write nonfiction articles, you already know which ones have universal appeal. Maybe that AIDs hospice is the first in the state. Perhaps that medical report is a breakthrough.

Examine your article with a cold, hard eye. Is it universal in theme? Is it focused? Do you incorporate quotes from authorities on the subject?

If your article is narrow enough in focus, it could qualify for a specialized award. I received one from the Lupus Foundation of America, for writing about the disease when few reporters did. I won another from the Independent Colleges and Schools for writing about the role of vocational education back when many assumed that a four-year degree was essential to success.

Focus Your Writing

The best sources for article contests are Writer's Digest magazine, Writers Market, the National Writers Association (which has an annual contest) or any other trade or consumer publication you read on a regular basis.

FIRST-CLASS FICTION

Writing fiction is tough, but there are a number of contests to add to your credits and help you gain the attention of editors. Not all of them require a great deal of time on your part. How long does it take to concoct a prize-winning story of 250 words? If yours is good enough, it could qualify for the World's Best Short, Short Story Contest, sponsored by Florida State University. The Hemingway and Dark and Stormy Night contests are other sources for good, short, quirky fiction.

The Hemingway competition rewards the best, and usually the funniest imitations of Hemingway's short stories and novels. The Dark-and-Stormy contest, based in San Jose, Calif., rewards and publishes the opening paragraphs of the worst books ever written. Both give you a reason to practice your very best worst within a focused format.

The National Writers Association sponsors annual fiction and novel contests, with real live loot for prizes. Writer's Digest magazine also sponsors an annual contest.

Many short-fiction contests limit word lengths to around 2,000. Judges look for clean writing, single viewpoints, conflict and a character who is somehow changed, whether or not the change is something the character realizes.

Novel contests come two ways. The first type requires your completed novel. Study the rules, study past winners and submit accordingly.

The second type requires you to submit a few chapters, usually three, and a synopsis.

As you will soon learn, the synopsis is the most boring piece of writing you will ever execute. Read the next chapter on how to do that, then write three clean chapters that define your characters and cut to the chase. Don't be afraid to underwrite.

Try to find an original focus and pick a sympathetic viewpoint character. Create conflict in the first chapter and build on it. Read Jack Bickham's book, "Scene & Structure." Study novels that work.

Does your novel hook the reader, reveal character and push the story forward with few flashbacks? How would you rate it against your favorite novel? Again, be as brutal as a contest judge will be.

Excellent sources for fiction contests are Writer's Market, Writer's Digest, and Poets & Writers magazines.

HOW MUCH TO PAY

Entry fees are the ugly realities of most writing contests. Some are reasonable. Others are ridiculous. This is the time that you must be the judge.

Don't kid yourself into thinking that paying a hefty entry fee will purchase a prize. Avoid contests that require you to buy a book in order to appear in it.

Even the biggest rip-off contest has to award its advertised prizes. Some writers enter them, knowing they won't buy the book but willing to take a chance on big money. I've done it, and I've won. On one occasion, I almost threw away the check because I thought it was another enticement to buy the "anthology." I wouldn't enter such a contest today, for any amount of money.

Try to let your common sense control your greed. Why tempt yourself with constant order forms for books you could never use as credits? Why support so-called publishers who might pay you but make their money from unsuspecting writers? If you're good, you'll find the right contest.

THE HANDFUL OF FINALISTS

A short story by a writer I know and respect won the Writer's Digest grand prize in 1993. In 1994, out of approximately 13,000 entrants, another story by her placed 24th. A fluke? A matter of luck? Hardly.

I believe that a small handful of writers are always the finalists in just about every contest. These people have craft and focus. Whether or not they place first or 10th depends on the inclination, bias and taste of the final judge. Getting into that handful is a matter of ability. You have to come across as a pro.

You can do it with theme. You can do it with subject matter and emotional appeal. Better yet, you can do it with focus.

You can't control who is judging you. It comes down to personal preference in the long run. All you can control is getting yourself into that handful. If you don't get there, you won't have a chance.

SUMMARY

A writing contest can earn you editorial attention, money, validation, and it can provide the all-important deadline every writer needs. Excellent contest sources are Writer's Digest magazine and Poets & Writers.

Credibility is as important than the cash amount of the prize. Don't enter a contest that requires entrants to purchase a book.

The manuscript with the most potential seldom wins a writing contest. Only complete manuscripts stand a chance. Simple technical rules can keep your manuscript from the finals. Most manuscripts entered in contests aren't that good.

Lack of a hook, a tendency to tell instead of show and technical problems are the three reason many entries don't make it. Past winners will teach you what works.

Check your title. Be certain it reflects your theme. Check your subject matter. Universal themes fare better. Be certain you've included emotional appeal in your entry.

Pay attention to the contest rules. Don't violate dictates of length or subject matter.

Specific guidelines exist for poetry contests, article contests and fiction contests. Know and follow them.

Consider entry fees and decide if the fee is worth what you might win. Don't submit to a rip-off contest that depends on the money of inexperienced writers who must buy the contest anthology to appear in it.

A small handful of writers always show up as finalists in most contests. Where they place depends on the judges, but they almost always appear in the top percentage. Getting into that handful is a matter of focus, and if you're serious about winning a writing contest, it is your goal.

ASSIGNMENT

1. Evaluate your entry before you submit, in terms of title, subject matter and emotional appeal.

2. Is this a real contest or a rip-off contest? Is the entry fee, if any, reasonable? Will you have to buy a book to see your work in print?

3. Have you chosen your best work and rewritten it? It's better to submit one good piece that six mediocre ones.

4. Have you studied and highlighted the contest guidelines? Is the word count correct? Does your subject matter reflect what the judges say they want?

5. Is the theme universal? Can other entrants understand why this one should be the winner?

6. Have you chosen a fresh slant? Are you looking at the theme in a unique way, with a unique vision?

7. Are the mechanics correct? If your manuscript is supposed to be double-spaced, is it? Have you checked and re-checked for spelling and punctuation?

8. Have you chosen a title that reflects the theme of the piece?

9. Have you ended the piece with your best line, regardless of how subtle it might be?

10. When you read the piece aloud, does it sound fresh and alive? Is this something you would read if you hadn't written it?

11. Have you submitted the entry so that it will arrive in plenty of time? Have you included an SASE if one is required?

In Appendix II, You'll find judge's cheat sheets you can use to rate your own manuscipts.

Entering contests is only one way to market your work. In the next chapter, we'll explore the marketing tools you must have, from the only query letter you'll ever need to write, to that dreaded synopsis every writer fears.

Many of my students think this is the reason they're taking my class. As a result, I used to teach marketing first. There's no reason to learn marketing, however, until you have a finished piece to sell. Now you do, so now it's time.

CHAPTER TEN

MARKETING TOOLS: QUERY, BLURB, OUTLINE, SUMMARY AND THAT DREADED SYNOPSIS

Now that you know how to focus a manuscript, you can just ship it off to The New Yorker or Reader's Digest, right? Sorry. As much as you may have come to hate the word, focus is as important in selling as it is to writing.

First, you need a marketable work, or in the case of nonfiction, a marketable idea. You have to write, rewrite, suffer and sweat until that piece is the best it can be. Then, using the tools you will find in this chapter, you must connect with the editor most likely to buy it.

MARKETING ENERGY

Selling is easy compared to crafting a finished article or story. One writer compared the feeling of sending out his novel to that of having a 20-pound weight lifted from him. Another told me that after she mailed her short story, she felt a burst of energy that lasted several days. That's marketing energy.

It makes you want to run home and get the mail every night of your life. You feel good about yourself and optimistic about the future. Enjoy this burst of energy and use it to push yourself into your next project.

THE REALITY OF REJECTION

Fact. You can't get published without rejection. Two maladies related to this unpleasant fact of the writing life are rejection fear, which often results in an inability to mail your manuscripts, and rejection depression, which occurs when you take the rejection personally.

Rejection fear manifests itself when you receive a go-ahead from an editor but just can't find time for that final rewrite before you mail your piece. It's probably the culprit lurking beneath your new-found fondness for television sit-coms when you know you should be addressing envelopes.

Remember, rejection is just a step toward publication. Most writers fail before they succeed. Count each rejection as one more step toward your goal.

If you think rejection fear is bad, just wait until you experience rejection depression. I once lived with a returned manuscript for an entire weekend before I could bring myself to open the envelope. That's rejection depression at its worse. Don't be this stupid. Your work, not you, was rejected, and for any number of reasons that may have nothing to do with your ability as a writer.

The best preventative for both of these maladies is a number of manuscripts in the mail. That way, your hope won't be centered on just one story or just one editorial response.

Address and stamp several envelopes to other publications. If you get a rejection, shove the manuscript into one of those waiting envelopes and mail it the same day.

THE FIRST STEP

As you already know by now, you'll find extensive market listings in Writer's Market, an annual guide to publications, what they pay, what they want and how to break in.

Writer's Digest magazine, and numerous smaller magazines and writers' clubs also publish current market news. Subscribe. Join. Often just reading the market listings will give you ideas for new articles or stories.

THE ONLY QUERY LETTER YOU'LL EVER NEED TO WRITE

Query Letter. Sounds pretty esoteric, doesn't it? You know you need one to sell, but you haven't the slightest idea how to address this editor, this person, you've never met. Should you be chatty, formal? Should you include a resume?

Well, pretend for a moment that you're an editor, any editor. This one, perhaps. It's 8:30 Monday morning, and your second cup of coffee tastes as bitter as the first. You need to dig up five more articles for the quarterly magazine you edit, preferably before noon. Your favorite free-lancers are busy on other projects, so you're stuck with the slush pile.

You reach down and pick up the first envelope. Cute little squirrel stickers decorate the front. The manuscript is addressed to "Editor." Would you open it?

Focus Your Writing

The next envelope looks more promising. You open it and begin reading. "Good morning," it begins. A little cheerful, but you're desperate, remember. "Would you be interested in considering 'Eric and Jill,' my short-story of 1,500 words? The story is set..." Fiction. Would you read on? Are you feeling cranky? Remember this feeling when you sit down to write your own query letter.

That's all you have to do. Just put yourself in the editor's chair, complete with deadline, workload and that second cup of lousy coffee; then, ask yourself what type of letter you'd like to receive. Probably not the brilliant, pun-laden examples you see in how-to articles, right?

I've never been able to figure out why most published examples of query letters make the process appear far more difficult than it is. Maybe because most effective query letters aren't all that exciting.

Exciting isn't the point. Effective is. Forget about being clever and remind yourself that you are one human writing to another about an idea that might well benefit both of you not to mention the reader to whom you targeted that idea in the first place.

Your letter should be short, concise, probably no longer than one single-spaced page. Since it will demonstrate your skill as a writer, it should be well-written, clean and lean. Once you've created this perfect query letter, you can simply substitute titles and concepts. The initial ingredients will remain the same.

Some writers vary their queries based on the style of the publication. This is a good trick if you don't overdo it. Most important is creating a businesslike, human letter that isn't stilted or gushy.

FOUR PARTS OF YOUR QUERY LETTER

The effective query letter contains four parts: Purpose, Content, Credits, Close.

Bonnie Hearn

1. The first part defines the **purpose**. It also includes the title of the piece. Some writers mention word length, and that's fine. I don't, because, based on the needs of the editor, length can change.

2. The next one or two paragraphs describe the **content** of the article. Don't ramble. Just tell the editor the focus of your article and why it will appeal to readers.

3. The next paragraph states your **credits**, either as a writer or as a person qualified to write about your proposed subject. If you don't have any, just omit the paragraph. If you have received a major award or placed in a national competition, say so.

Not this: "This essay received eighth honorable mention in the St. Louis Scribbler's annual contest." More like this: "The essay was a winner in the National Writers Association's annual contest last year."

4. In your **close**, state that you will be happy to provide the article on speculation, which means that you understand it may not be purchased.

The final close tells the editor that you look forward to hearing from him or her. You don't have to say that you have enclosed an SASE, although, of course, you have. The editor isn't blind.

Here is an example of a query letter that works for me. I include it, not because I think it's brilliant, but because it demonstrates how simple and straightforward such a query can be. Besides, I didn't have to worry about getting permission from the author.

Focus Your Writing

Leslie Winegar, Publisher
CT Publishing Company
PO Box 99217
Redding, California 96099-2197

Dear Leslie Winegar,

I am a newspaper editor and published writer in search of a publisher for my book, "Focus Your Writing." The book shows the beginning and published writer how to increase sales by using the concept of focus.

A chapter from it was published by Writer's Digest magazine last June. Another appeared in the National Writers Association magazine, Authorship.

Most writers who fail do so because of lack of focus, not lack of talent. While some articles touch on the importance of focus, no one has written a book on how to use it as a tool in crafting marketable fiction and nonfiction.

Since 1982, I have worked as an editor for The Fresno Bee, a daily newspaper with approximately 350,000 readers. My own articles and fiction appear regularly in magazines such as Family Circle, Good Housekeeping, Writer's Digest and literary publications such as Pig Iron.

I teach writing, judge major writing contests and speak at many conferences. I feel my teaching, articles and speaking engagements alone would create a market for the book.

Most of all, I am convinced that focus will be an important concept in the '90s and that my book will help writers improve their approach and increase their sales. If you are willing to look at the manuscript, I would be happy to send part or all of it to you at once.

I look forward to hearing from you.

Best regards,

Once you have a query that pleases you, continue to send it out until an editor responds. Count on 10 to 20 queries for one article when you're just starting.

Being rejected by a single editor doesn't mean your idea stinks. The magazine might have recently published an article on a similar theme (although if you researched the publication, you'd know that before you queried). If your query fails to *consistently* generate a positive response, take a critical look at it. Is it focused, well-written, succinct?

Also study the kind of rejections you're receiving. Form letters? Not a good sign. If you've truly crafted a focused query, and if you have a fresh idea that is slanted to the publication, the right editor will request to see more.

THE COVER LETTER

A cover letter is just that—something that *covers* whatever else is riding along with it. Whether you're writing short stories or nonfiction, you need only two cover letters in your bag of tricks. Use the first when you're submitting material an editor has requested in response to your query letter. Use the second when you're submitting the complete piece, fiction or nonfiction, to an editor who doesn't require queries.

The first reminds the editor that she's given you a go-ahead. As with your initial query, it includes Purpose, Content, Credits, Close.

Focus Your Writing

> *Dear Mr. X,*
>
> *Thank you for agreeing to read my enclosed manuscript.* **(PURPOSE)**.
>
> *As you may recall, the article will show even a novice how to roast the finest gourmet coffee for less than half the price of supermarket beans.* **(CONTENT)**.
>
> *Although I've written and read many food articles, I believe that mine is the first to deal with this particular slant.* **(CREDITS)**.
>
> *I hope you like the article, and I look forward to hearing from you.* **(CLOSE)**.
>
> Best regards,

When you send requested material, mark your envelope with the words REQUESTED MATERIAL, and don't forget to include a self-addressed, stamped envelope (SASE).

Use the second cover letter for short stories or unsolicited articles for which publishers don't require queries.

> *Dear Ms. XXXX,*
>
> *Enclosed is an article I feel will be of interest to your readers.*
>
> *As you may know, home-roasting is gaining in popularity with coffee lovers in California. My article shows how anyone can roast his or her own coffee beans at home.*
>
> *I am a published article writer of food articles. My credits include Gourmet and Bon Appetit magazines.*
>
> *I hope you like the article, and I look forward to hearing from you.*
>
> Best regards,

Many markets don't require a query. Do your research. Query letters are never necessary for short stories. A fiction editor must see the final product in order to judge it.

If you are submitting a short story, use this version of the second cover letter.

Dear Mr. or Ms. X,

Enclosed is a manuscript I feel will be of interest to your readers. **(PURPOSE. Omit content for fiction. Let the story speak for itself.)**

"Title" was recently published in a local literary magazine. I'm hoping that you will consider it worthy of a larger audience. **(CREDITS, if appropriate.)**

I am a published free-lance writer and would welcome any comments, positive or negative, that you might have. **(CLOSE, a strong one. You've asked for editorial input.)**

I look forward to hearing from you.

Best regards,

Many writers don't include cover letters, and many pieces sell without them. That's your choice. Maybe it's a quirk, but something about even the shortest letter makes me stop for a moment and remember that these pages I'm about to read were sent to me by a real, live person. Am I more likely to read a submission accompanied by a cover letter? I don't know. I do know that when a writer has gone to the trouble to write and sign a letter, I'd feel rude if I didn't at least take a peek at the accompanying manuscript.

Focus Your Writing

BASICS OF THE BLURB

Although most editors won't recognize it as such, a blurb can be a great sales tool for that novel you're trying to sell. Lucky for you. Try passing the blurb off as a short synopsis with your query letter to an agent or publisher.

Never call it by its true name. Just say: *Enclosed is a short synopsis of my novel, TITLE, which I hope you will consider for publication.* Play your cards right, and no one will know that you slipped in a blurb instead.

A true blurb is advertising copy. It reads, not like your novel, but like the material that appears on the back covers of paperbacks to entice readers to buy them. Study the supermarket shelves, and you'll get the hang of it.

Usually, the blurb starts with a short, shocking statement that describes the story problem.

1. *Who killed Robin Black?*

    Or:

2. *They were the best of Mills College's graduating crop, but somewhere between graduation and their class reunion, something went terribly wrong.*

A blurb is written, double spaced, in the present tense. After the lead, you give short descriptions of your character(s) and their problems.

1. *Suspects aren't the problem: Robin's former boss who'd been her lover; her long-suffering banker husband, her estranged sister. The problem is where Joe Blow should start before Robin's killer is able to entrap another unsuspecting model.*

    Or:

2. *Too many years had passed since the promise of graduation and the unfolding freedom of the '60s. Janie had married well, if one overlooked the occasional bruises. Always-slender Marie was now painfully thin, but a top model, they told each other at holiday gatherings. Althea, always the star, had made it in Hollywood, thanks to Janie's husband, a brutal but successful producer.*

Then you cut to the situation on which your plot hinges.

1. *When Joe's lover, Brenda, disappears, he realizes that he must risk his own life to confront the one person who can help him.*

Or:

2. *At their 10-year class reunion, tragedy strikes, and when one of the group is murdered, the remaining friends must deal with the realities of their own lives.*

Let's take a look at how these ingredients can contribute to a successful blurb for both of our imaginary stories.

1. *Who killed Robin Black?*
Suspects aren't the problem: Robin's former boss who'd been her lover; her long-suffering banker husband, her estranged sister. The problem is where Joe Blow should start before Robin's killer is able to entrap another unsuspecting model.

When Joe's lover, Brenda, disappears, he realizes that he must risk his own life to confront the one person who can help him.

Or:

Focus Your Writing

2. They were the best of Mills College's graduating crop, but somewhere between graduation and their class reunion, something went terribly wrong.

Too many years had passed since the promise of graduation and the unfolding freedom of the '60s. Janie had married well, if one overlooked the occasional bruises. Always-slender Marie was now painfully thin, but a top model, they told each other at holiday gatherings. Althea, always the star, had made it in Hollywood, thanks to Janie's husband, a brutal but successful producer.

At their 10-year class reunion, tragedy strikes, and when one of the group is murdered, the remaining friends must deal with the realities of their own lives.

While character definitions can be longer, and often should be, a basic blurb should be no more than two or three pages. Try to tell your story as an ad writer would, with as few words as possible.

THE DREADED SYNOPSIS

As you have already surmised, the synopsis is the most boring piece of writing you'll ever attempt. Place it at the back of your submission, and when you write it, try to concentrate on action.

A published novelist I know created a 60-page synopsis to market a mainstream book with (what I thought was) tremendous potential. She never sold that novel, and I always wondered if the synopsis might be part of the reason. Sixty pages can look pretty darn formidable to an editor with limited reading time.

Try to keep your synopsis to around 12 double-spaced pages. Start with the protagonist and his/her problem. Follow the plot of the story right to the end. Don't omit the conclusion as beginning writers often do. It is the mark of an amateur, and it makes editors crazy.

A synopsis is often required when you're submitting the first few chapters of a novel to an editor or agent. If it's your first contact with this person, feel free to substitute a blurb.

THE SUMMARY

Consider your summary the nonfiction version of a blurb. Again, it's ad copy. Pretend you're reading the back cover of your book. What promises can you make? Are they as enticing as these from "20 Master Plots (And How to Build Them)" by Ronald B. Tobias?

> *Here you'll find twenty plots discussed and analyzed plots that recur through all fiction, no matter what the genre. You'll learn how a successful plot integrates all elements of a story, and how to use these plots effectively in your own work...*
>
> *You'll learn that an effective plot is...*
> - *diffusive it permeates all the atoms of your fiction.*
> - *a process, not an object.*
> - *dynamic, not static.*
>
> *The point of this book isn't to give you a rundown of twenty master plots that you simply choose from for your next story. Instead, this book shows you how to develop plot in fiction. It also shows you how to apply any subject matter, so you develop plot evenly and effectively. As a result, your fiction will be effective as well.*

Focus Your Writing

CHAPTER-BY-CHAPTER OUTLINE

A chapter-by-chapter outline is part of the nonfiction book proposal you send to an editor or agent. It runs about four double-spaced pages, and it usually includes one paragraph for each chapter, with a catchy chapter heading at the top.

This outline has to be written with the energy of a blurb and the substance of a serious outline, the kind you had to turn out for that god-awful research paper back in English 1A. The editor must know what's contained in each chapter but must also be convinced that the material won't be dry and boring to the reader. The tables of contents in many books started out as chapter outlines.

THE AGENT LETTER, NOVEL, NONFICTION

Use this tool for books only. It should be a one-page, single-spaced letter.

> *Dear Ms. Jones,*
>
> *I am a published writer in search of an agent. My novel, TITLE, is a mystery set in the year 2046.* **(Include credits, if you have them.)**
>
> *Enclosed are the first chapter and a short synopsis of the book. If you are interested in seeing the completed manuscript, I would be happy to send it to you at once.*
>
> *I look forward to hearing from you.*
>
> *Best regards,*

Bonnie Hearn

THE BOOK PROPOSAL, NONFICTION

Include, in this order, the letter, summary, chapter outline, introduction, first chapter, up to 20 pages, possibly a published clip or two of articles you have published, and SASE.

Some of the best advice I've ever seen on this subject was in a letter written to one of my students by a successful New York agent. I'm reprinting part of it, without permission, mind you, but with enough changes that I don't think my doing so will harm either party.

> *Dear Ms. X,*
>
> *After reviewing TITLE, I like what I have seen thus far.*
>
> *For a nonfiction book, however, I prefer to present a proposal, not a completed manuscript. The proposal should contain the following.*
>
> *First, you must provide an introduction that will briefly discuss your premise. Then, you need a page of biographical information. An editor will want to see your credentials in order to know if you can write this book.*
>
> *There should also be a chapter-by-chapter outline and one or two chapters with the charts and questionnaires you mentioned. You should state where these will appear in the book.*
>
> *If you provide me with this information, and if it is what I believe it is, I will then want to take your book on for representation.*

THE BOOK PROPOSAL, FICTION

Include, in this order, the letter, blurb (which you will call a short synopsis), first chapter, and SASE.

Know that selling your novel *sans* agent may prove frustrating. If you're adamant about doing it yourself, you'd better be a genre writer or a genius, preferably the latter.

Go ahead, if you must. Or consider purchasing Writer's Digest Books' annual "Guide to Literary Agents & Art/Photo Reps."

AGENT PROPOSAL

Based on requirements (and they vary), include, in this order, the agent letter, blurb or summary, the first 50 pages, and SASE.

Don't forget your telephone number. If you manage to pique an agent's interest, he'll probably want to talk to you now.

New York agent Nancy Yost said she prefers to receive a first chapter with an initial query letter.

"If I'm interested in the idea, I don't want to wait to see the material," she said.

This is the way most busy agents operate. They can tell at a glance if the writing works, and if the material is right for them. If it is, they reach for the phone.

POETRY

Send a cover letter, three to 10 poems, depending on requirements, and SASE. Some poetry magazines may request a biography. If so, go easy and try to mention only your important past credits.

Bonnie Hearn

THE RULE OF TWELVE AND OTHER SUPERSTITIONS

We writers are superstitious. We have to believe in luck if we are to continue facing that blank page every day. I sincerely believe that if I have 10, not nine, not 11 manuscripts in the mail at any given time, I will make a sale. The Rule of Twelve is a variation on my personal theme.

According to the Rule of Twelve, a writer needs 12 manuscripts in the mail at any given time. Some writers have sworn, in print, at that, that they couldn't sell until they had that magic number out there.

One of my students made her first two sales because, after my Rule-of-Twelve lecture, she had decided to scout out two additional markets in addition to the 10 to which she had already submitted. The last two bought. The other 10 didn't.

Needless to say, my student's now a believer. I'm not, but I share this superstition with you as I shared it with her. Maybe like my student, you'll get lucky. At least you'll have 12—not one, not two possible publishers looking at your work.

I do believe that once you start selling, you get a feeling for how many "nos" you need to get one "yes." That is your real Rule of Twelve or Law of Twenty. So you get a rejection. You know you're one step closer to that magic number, whatever it may be. In order to publish, you have to get rejections. Thus, each one brings you that much closer to publication.

When a former student phoned me recently, I told her how some of my current students were publishing using the Rule of Twelve.

"That's crazy," she said. "I couldn't go through all that rejection."

I asked about the travel article she had written in class. How many times she had sent it out?

"Well, not 12 times. I just couldn't go through that."

"How many times?"

"Well," she began. "Actually, I never sent it out. I've been really busy."

Don't do this to yourself. You'll never publish if you won't or can't submit what you write.

Michael, a disc jockey/crime-story writer phoned me, after repeated rejections, to report that he'd received four more that day.

As I attempted to console him, he interrupted me.

"And one acceptance," he said.

The first short story he had written for my class, one he'd rewritten nine times in eight weeks, had sold, after 11 rejections, to Oui magazine, circulation 1 million. Not bad for a first story. The secret? Simple. Michael, a gifted, uneducated guy from the streets, had lived with rejection his entire life.

"Rejection, man. It's no big deal," he used to tell me. I believed him (and I also kind of liked the way he called me "man"). His life on the streets had given Michael the guts to keep sending that story out, whatever the consequences. It wasn't a fluke, either. He wrote and sold four more stories that year.

Superstitions aside, having a number of manuscripts in the mail is good for you as a writer. A number of editors have a chance to read and possibly comment on your work. You aren't risking all your emotional energy on that one manuscript and that one publication. You have a reason to rush to the mailbox each night.

SIMULTANEOUS SUBMISSIONS: THE TRUTH

Editors frown in print about this nefarious habit. Many writing teachers insist you'll be blackballed if you do it, but their admonitions are really just more hocus pocus. The truth about submitting to more than one publisher at a time is that, love it or hate it, everybody does it.

Why should you let an editor hold onto your query letter or article until it's no longer fresh? Is that editor really going to respect you any more because you're willing or stupid enough to wait months to sell one manuscript?

"But what if more than one editor wants to buy it?" the beginning writer often asks.

Great. Write to the other publication(s). Say that you've sold the piece and are withdrawing it from consideration. The editor will appreciate your informing her, and she might even act faster the next time you submit.

The manuscript belongs to you until you sell it. The more you submit it to target publications, the better your chances. The minute someone gives you money for it, the manuscript is theirs (based on whatever rights they purchase, of course).

I know. I know. You've read all those articles by editors, telling you to notify them if you multiple submit. If you were an editor, how would *you* regard such a submission? Right. Me, too.

Editors know only what *they* need (a massive collection of uncommitted manuscripts), not what *you* need (a commitment. Now).

Let me confess. As an editor, I've held onto manuscripts, honestly intending to publish them, then had to reject them months later, because of a change in editorial concept.

As a writer, I've had to wait as long as two years to see an article of mine in print. I've sold a 2,000-word article to a dollar-a-word magazine and received $200 after the new editor trimmed it. Fortunately I'd already sold that article, in its entirety, to said magazine's competition.

How did I feel about that? How would you feel if you had a check for $2,000 in one hand, and a check for $200 in the other? How would you feel if you'd never mailed off the second article and had only $200 to show for the time and energy you had put into the piece?

The only way to find out what your writing is worth is to submit to a number of publications. It's called simultaneous submission, and there's not a thing wrong with it. Simultaneous submission puts the ball in your court. It returns control to you. It allows you to browse, the way editors do, and decide what you like and what you don't.

All of this happens before you actually connect with a publisher, of course. Once that occurs, you're married. Your relationship with the publisher is indeed a marriage. The minute you say, "I do," you're committed.

One of my students called me when she received a contract from an international fiction market for a short story she had written.

"What should I do?" she asked. "I've also submitted it to Atlantic magazine, and I'd rather publish there."

This was an unpublished writer speaking. It was her first short story in which any market had indicated an interest, and she was sitting on a contract hoping for pie in the Atlantic sky.

I told her to sign the contract and go out and celebrate. Needless to say, Atlantic did not buy her story.

When you send a query or an article, you're saying that you want to appear in that magazine, not Atlantic, not Cosmopolitan. When you receive an acceptance, sign that contract, endorse that check and be grateful. As you gain more experience, you can get pickier about the markets you select. At the beginning, when establishing an history of publication is your goal, submit to as many magazines as possible —simultaneously, of course.

The way you market your work is not that editor's business. His or her job is to determine whether or not your article will fit the needs of the publication, and if so, to buy it right now.

When I receive a focused, marketable piece from a writer, I assume that writer is smart enough to submit the article to other editors as well. We editors have no right to hang onto marketable manuscripts while we try to decide whether or not we want to buy them. Simultaneous submission is the only way writers can protect themselves from those of us who aren't up to the jobs and the manuscripts entrusted to us.

SUMMARY

Marketing is both an exciting and frustrating part of writing—exciting because you're actually seeking an editorial response, and frustrating because you're risking rejection.

Let the excitement push you into a new project, and know that rejection is just one of the steps to publication.

A query letter should include purpose, content, credits and close. Use queries only when your target publication requests them. Otherwise, send the entire manuscript with a cover letter. Count on 10 to 20 queries for one article when you're first submitting.

Use a cover letter when submitting fiction, when submitting nonfiction to a publication that does not require a query letter and when submitting a complete manuscript to an editor who has requested it.

Try using a fast-paced blurb instead of a full-blown synopsis when marketing a novel. Use the same technique when crafting a summary of a nonfiction book, or use the table of contents in place of a chapter-by-chapter outline.

A nonfiction book proposal should include, a one-page, single-spaced letter, summary, chapter outline, introduction, first chapter, up to 20 pages, published clips and SASE.

A novel proposal should include a one-page, single-spaced letter, blurb, first chapter and SASE.

Based on requirements, an agent proposal should include a one-page, single-spaced letter, blurb or summary, the first 50 pages and SASE. Be sure to include your phone number or e-mail.

Poetry submissions should consist of a cover letter, three to 10 poems and SASE.

Whether you believe in the Rule of Twelve (that you must have 12 manuscripts in the mail in order to sell), or your own rule, you'll feel better if you submit numerous manuscripts to numerous editors. This means multiple submission, which is more common than some editors would have you believe. Once you connect with a publisher, however, you are committed. Sign your contract and congratulate yourself.

ASSIGNMENT

1. Write a query letter for a specific article to a specific publication. Be certain that it includes: purpose, contents, credits (if applicable) and close.

2. Wait a few hours, then read the letter again. Carefully. Is it the best writing you're capable of producing?

3. Assemble the appropriate submission package for the work you're attempting to sell. Check it against the information in this chapter.

4. Send it out, 10 times, 12 times, 20 times, as many times as it takes. If you receive personal comments on rejection letters, consider them but wait until you have at least 20 or 30 rejections before you consider rewriting.

Now that you're seriously marketing your work, the time you spend doing that will conflict with the time you spend writing and editing. In the next chapter, you'll find out how to organize and balance the four parts of your job as a writer.

CHAPTER ELEVEN

YOUR TIME AS A WRITER (AND WHAT IT'S WORTH)

Your time as a writer is all you have. Before you even begin to think about publishing, you have to free up some hours.

First of all, turn off the television. Do you have any idea how many hours you spend in front of it when you could be writing, thinking, not to mention, living your life?

One of my talented students watched a lot of TV. She claimed she turned it on when she got up, and I seriously wonder when she turned it off. She said it kept her company. Visiting her was distracting. I could always hear the TV buzzing away in the background. Somehow, I could hear it in her work as well. Strangely enough, she was never quite *there*. Her work was never quite focused.

I know I sound like an evangelist, but I once wrote television commercials. I understand the medium. It's the drug of escape, and regardless of how much you rationalize, it can only hurt your writing. Worse, it can rob you of precious time. Try it my way, for at least a week. Sequester yourself away from this powerful drug. Just say *Later*.

Next, forget that you own a telephone. Add up the minutes you spend on the phone, and you just might want to have it ripped out. Writers like to talk. It's better than facing that lonely task of putting words on paper. Buy an answering machine. Return the calls that really need returning when you choose to.

Once you've evaluated your time as a writer, you have to decide how many hours a week you can work toward your goal. Don't exaggerate.

What you have to do is look at one week in your life. You've already cut out the two biggest time wasters, the TV and the phone. If you eliminate nothing else, you now have some extra space in your life. Here's how to use it.

YOUR FOUR JOBS AS A WRITER

When you evaluate how much time you can spend as a writer, you must first realize that writing is only one of four jobs you must perform in order to publish. You must look at that free block of time, whether two hours or 20, and divide it like a pie into four uneven slices.

1. The first is **production**. At some point during your week, you must write, not re-write, not edit. As a writer, you owe yourself some heavy-duty creative time for just writing.

2. The next slice of your weekly time chunk is for **editing**. While writing is a creative, right-brain process, editing is deadly left-brain stuff. This is when you sit down with your creation and coldly strip and cut anything that doesn't work. This editing process does not count as production. You need to do both, but not at once.

As we've already discussed, you'll be frustrated if you try to write and edit in one session. Don't attempt it. Realize that these are two separate jobs, to be performed at two different times during your writer's week.

3. The third slice must be spent ***marketing***. This is when you write query and cover letters, when you buy stamps and mail your manuscripts. Writing and editing are not enough. You must also sell.

4. The fourth slice is one that receives far too much attention. ***Research***. Many writers avoid the other three tasks to concentrate on it. Research is an excellent way to avoid the real work of writing.

You don't need much initial research when you're writing or editing. Just leave a blank when you need to fill in some data. Don't dwell on it. The research comes in once the manuscript is nearly finished. At that point, you'll know exactly what you need, based on the focus of your piece.

Consider reading as part of your research. If you take a writing class or read writing publications, count in the time as research hours.

Keep track of how many hours a week you spend on each of these: Production, editing, marketing, research. The slices won't be equal, and the size of each will vary depending on your given focus.

You must have all four, especially the first three, and you must know how many hours in your week you can set aside to devote to them.

Focus Your Writing

SO, WHAT'S IT WORTH?

Now that you know how much time you have to be a writer and how that time must be spent, you need to know how much it is worth.

This is the part few writers like to discuss. It seems rude, doesn't it, to just blurt out to the closest published writer, "How much do you earn, anyway?" Like many rude questions, it's an important one.

According to a survey in 1993, Princeton Survey Research Associates on behalf of the Author's Relief Fund, found that from January to June of that year, the survey showed a median income of $3,058 based on an average of 26 hours per week spent writing. That boils down to an hourly wage of $4.61.

The survey is based on 637 responses to questionnaires mailed to 1,000 members of the Author's Guild and the Dramatists Guild. It's said that the average free-lance writer in the United States earns less than $9,000 annually. While that may be true, I know many who earn much more. I do, even in a bad year.

The average book advance is from $5,000 to $12,000, but you won't get all of it at once. Genre (category) novels, such as romances and westerns, often earn less. Mainstreams receive more, especially if you're Danielle Steel or Stephen King, genre writers, whose sales shot them to mainstream status.

With the depressed state of today's short-story markets, many fiction writers decide to gamble on a novel. Yet, most of my novelist friends have to keep their day jobs. One only began making good money after he changed agents and started selling his books to international publishers.

The odds for nonfiction writers are a little better. Consider the average novel advance against the numerous national publications that pay $1 or more per word for articles.

Bonnie Hearn

FOR LOVE OR MONEY?

Am I saying, "Don't quit your day job?" Not unless you have more nerve than I (or a trust fund). Those of us who free-lance at our newspaper share a common joke. "There's no such thing as a free lunch or a cushy free-lance job."

Each time one of us lands what looks like an easy-money job, we enjoy it for what it's worth at the time, knowing that next week or next month, the client will want more than we can provide, or that the new, wonderful and endless budget will suddenly run out.

Even writing for top-paying magazines provides no more financial security than buying a lottery ticket. Money from writing arrives when you least expect it, which can be nice if you weren't counting on it for the car payment three months before. Publications that pay on acceptance have varying ideas about when that moment of acceptance occurs. Those scoundrels who pay on "publication" sometimes never get around to the actual act.

Trend-guessing doesn't help either. Trying to predict a trend that will make your book the next "Bridges of Madison County" is riskier than betting on who's going to win the next presidential election. What's worse, writing doesn't follow the rules of other businesses, although some writers comfort themselves by pretending that it does. That piece you concocted from leftover research from an opus may earn five times the amount of the original.

In "A Writer's Guide to Money," published in the 1995 Writer's Market, Gary Provost again says it best.

>   ...Rule number one about writing and money is that fair has nothing to do with it. Nobody is going to buy your book, short story or magazine article just because you worked really hard. 'A fair day's pay for a fair day's work' doesn't apply to writing for a living...

Focus Your Writing

> *...Did you use your research material in three other articles, thus making your time more cost effective, or is this article the only one you will write on the subject? (Editors) don't care. You are going to get paid what your work is worth to the editor, not what it is worth to you...*

Don't let any of these realities make you crazy, and don't try to crank out formula anything. If money were your focus, you'd have become a stock broker or gone into real estate. You're a gambler, a dreamer, a creative person, and if you're like most of us, you probably wouldn't change now.

Be aware of the markets and the trends, but write for the sheer joy of it, for what you personally gain from putting those words on paper.

DEVELOP YOUR BASE

In order to make money as a writer, you need a consistent base of clients/publications, not just one-shot sales. You need to develop relationships with editors, so that you can forget the rules and just drop a note or pick up the phone when you have an idea.

One of my students began selling articles to our newspaper by way of formal query letters. Finally, she graduated to timid telephone calls, where she would suggest an idea for an article. As she proved herself, we started to count on her to come through when we needed a piece. Sometimes we even called her. One day at lunch, she scribbled, in pencil, as we ate with two other writers.

"What are you doing?" I asked.

"Just jotting down some ideas for your real estate section," she said, looking up from her chow mein.

I took her list back to work with me and handed it to my manager, who suggested that we give my student the go-ahead to write several of the articles.

When I phoned with the good news, I said, "If there were a contest for the worst possible query letter, you would win. Yours was scribbled in pencil, yet, and on notebook paper, complete with soy-sauce stains. What's the lesson there?"

"Maybe," she said, "that once you've established a relationship with an editor, the rules aren't as important as they once were."

She was right.

So, what will you earn as a free-lance writer? Again, you need to study Writer's Market. You also need to talk to people you know who have published.

Writer's Market will also tell you how much you can charge for a multitude of services ranging from advertising copywriting to ghost writing. Follow those guidelines, depending on where you live.

At our newspaper, a free-lance piece earns from $50 to $120, based on its length and how many sources are involved. A student of mine sold us a guest editorial piece for $100. I suggested he sell second rights to the story to our sister paper in another city. The other paper paid him $50 more than we did. The writer earned $250 for one article he wrote in my classroom.

Regardless of what you charge, try to give the client more than he or she expects. You don't want anyone saying or feeling that you were paid too much for a job. Make your presentation as professional as possible. Meet your deadline ahead of time. Offer to rewrite at no additional charge. Do all of this and you'll be able to charge whatever you want once you've proven yourself.

SUMMARY

Writing takes time. Start by getting rid of your two biggest wastes of time, the television and the telephone.

Your job as a writer includes, not just the actual act of writing, but also editing, marketing and research. Keep track of how many hours a week you spend on each.

Focus Your Writing

While the national averages for writing income are lower than $10,000, many writers earn far more. Anticipating trends is little help. Pretending writing is like any other business doesn't help much either. Be aware of the markets and trends but write for the joy and satisfaction you receive.

Develop a consistent base of clients and publications, not just one-time sales. Be professional. Meet deadlines. In short, prove yourself, and editors will want to work with you again and again.

ASSIGNMENT

1. Write yourself a solemn pledge. "For just one month, I will give up television and phone calls I can return at a later time." Write it down. Stick to it.

2. Break down your week as a writer into honest hours. How many hours can you give to production, editing, marketing and research?

3. Study Writer's Market. How much should you expect to be paid for your story? How many stories must you write in order to earn enough to make writing a viable profession for you?

4. Call local advertising agencies and newspapers. Ask point blank what they pay for free-lance submissions. Believe about half of what you hear.

5. Don't quit your day job. Yet.

Now that you know what to write and have an idea of what to charge, you're probably ready to network with other writers, join clubs and pursue causes. Maybe. In the next chapter, you'll find out the difference between a club and a con, and why most writing classes probably won't help you publish.

Focus Your Writing

Bonnie Hearn

CHAPTER TWELVE

CLASSES, CLUBS, CAUSES AND CONS

If I had known 30 years ago what I'm about to tell you right now, I would have saved myself about 10 years of unfocused wandering in search of the perfect writing class. Save yourself those 10 years I lost. Start by knowing that most writing classes won't get you published. They may even hinder the process.

Why? Two possible reasons are:

1. ***The teacher doesn't know enough.*** He may have a Ph.D. She may have published a dozen genre novels back when that genre was hot. If the teacher doesn't understand focus and marketing, the class may be nothing more than a club.

2. ***It's a rip-off.*** Sad to say, but a few writers who can't earn enough to make it on their books and articles alone decide to take the easy route. They cultivate suckers they can continue to stroke like human slot machines.

Focus Your Writing

At an early age, I accidentally ended up in a class taught by one of the finest poets of our time. He was an outrageous and brutal teacher. There was no room for dishonesty in his classroom. Those of us who could handle the criticism improved rapidly. Many of my fellow students are recognized poets today. The teacher has gone on to win two National Book Awards and has written poems that will live as long as there are people to read them.

Although I enrolled in other writing classes after that, I never again felt the honesty, unconditional approval and absolute terror I did in that man's classroom.

With exception of the gifted poet/professor, my real teachers were the editors for whom I wrote. They dispassionately carved away my prose to reveal the single idea hidden within. Although they may not have known it, they taught me focus, something few learn in any writing class.

Most of the classes with which I've been acquainted fall into four categories.

1. ***The stroke group***. Everyone's wonderful. Everyone will get published, as long as they keep on paying. The students are slot machines. The teacher, who usually has a few category novels to his or her credit, just keeps on pulling that handle.

Your family will do this for free. Do you really need the class?

2. ***The academic aerobics class***. The teacher hands you a book of Hemingway short stories and tells you to be creative. You do your best to imitate. The criticism is esoteric, and you go away doubting yourself.

As the stroke group builds you up, the academic aerobics class brings you down. While the stroke teacher promises that everyone can do it, the academic aerobics instructor suggests that it will take years of reading the classics, maybe even getting a master's degree.

3. *The sewing circle.* This is a basically harmless class, unless you're serious about publishing now. No one's in a hurry in this class, which is usually made up of long-time students working on pieces they started decades before.

Over the years, students have rubbed against each other like stones in a stream. The sharp ones are tossed out. Those who stay are rubbed even smoother. They bring their knitting and their cookies and visit with each other like the old friends they have become. The class is their hobby.

Some of them have stopped writing altogether, but they still pay their dues, telling themselves they'll get back to it when they have the time.

4. *The synergistic class.* Once in a great while, you may find a class like the one I took from the poet. Nobody flatters you. Other students offer sometimes brutal, usually helpful criticism. Comments from classmates, if they are allowed at all, are brief and focused, not esoteric or gushy.

The energy of the class is greater than the sum of its parts. The teacher speaks with a kind of authority it is difficult to doubt. You go away angry sometimes, but you always wake up with a good idea.

The right class must expand and develop you, not limit or frustrate you. A good teacher probably isn't in it for the money. He is probably writing and publishing in addition to teaching. If not, be careful. You'll be learning someone else's theory by way of someone else's theory. You want a teacher who can show you firsthand what editors expect.

One "editor/teacher" I know means well. She has a degree from Stanford. She cares, and she does her best to help her students. The problem is her lack of credits. Since she's never published and never worked as an editor for a publication of any kind, she can only guess when she does her well-intentioned, high-priced line edits.

Knowing grammar and spelling doesn't make you a writing teacher. Having published a novel doesn't make you a writing teacher. Needing extra money and talking a good game doesn't make you a writing teacher, and being a nice person most definitely doesn't make you a writing teacher.

A good teacher should have: a history of success, the ability to see what must be cut from the story, not just added to it, and the blatant honesty to say when a story works and when it doesn't.

EVALUATING A WRITING CLASS

I once sat in on what turned out to be a sewing circle writing class. During the course of the evening, as we gathered around the teacher's dining room table, I asked the regular students how long they'd been there.

Ten years, said one. Eleven years, another said. Eight, four, nine. None of them had published.

While the teacher was knowledgeable, she wasn't effective, and she certainly wasn't focused. One of her students finally published her novel—eight years later.

The novel had promise that first night I heard the student read from it, but in spite of the teacher's comments, I knew even then that it needed less, not more. Maybe the teacher knew it, as well. But when the bottom line is dollars and cents, it's better to keep on collecting those monthly bucks than to tell yourself and your gifted student she can publish now, not eight years from now.

Who's at fault when writing students still aren't publishing after one, five or more years of dutiful attendance? The misguided teachers? The unemployed editors and rip-off novelists posing as mentors? No. The writers, all of them, are at fault for continuing in classes they must know are failing them at a crucial level.

It's your responsibility to evaluate a class before you join. Most teachers will allow you to attend at least one session at no charge.

QUESTION THE TEACHER

Where is the class held? The teacher's home? That's all right, but it could be a cost-effective measure to extract as much profit as possible. An adult school? A university? These more neutral, impersonal settings might be better if you have the right teacher.

Where has the teacher published? What genre? Can you obtain copies? How much does he charge? How long has he been teaching, and how many writers has he helped publish? Where and for how much? How does he conduct the class? Is criticism fair, focused and accurate? Is it tough? It should be. Is it slanted to publication or a general philosophy?

QUESTION THE STUDENTS

How long have they been taking the class? What have they published? Where and for how much? Is there an equal mix of men and women in the class? Is anybody knitting or doing needlework? Are the critiques of fellow students on target? Is the atmosphere either too safe or too threatening? What books do these people read? What are their ambitions as writers?

QUESTION YOURSELF

Would you be comfortable here? That's not always a good sign. Better, would you be challenged here? Do you respect this teacher and his credentials? Do you leave the class wanting to write? Is the information imparted focused and easy to apply to your own work? Compared to other classes in the area, is this one worth the money?

Is the teacher someone you can trust, not as a friend, but as a mentor and role model? You have to trust that teacher 95 percent, at least. There has to be a ring of truth when he critiques your work. Kind words are great, and they'll keep you coming to class, but they won't get you published.

On the other hand, you don't need cruel or incorrect criticism from other students. Do you trust the teacher's ability to keep the comments from class members focused and on track?

ALTERNATIVES TO CLASSES

If you've looked around and not found a writing class to meet your needs, don't despair. Alternatives to classes include writing clubs, conferences, criticism services, books and critique groups. Even the worst of these might offer you more than spending years in the wrong class.

WRITING CLUBS

Your community probably has at least one writing club. Many are comprised of well-meaning types, who share cookies and glowing comments on boring writing.

Others are what I call the users and the losers. The club is made up of a few published writers who sell their books and collect speaking fees from their groupies. You want, not just a club, but a cause, an organization dedicated to writers and all they represent.

Some communities have them, and some don't. If not, consider joining a national group such as Romance Writers of America, Mystery Writers of America, Sisters In Crime, or a powerful regional group such as Southwest Writers Workshop in Albuquerque, NM, if only to get their magazine and the price breaks on their annual conference.

Most good writers' groups are informal. They grow out of classes or book signings or readings. That's one more reason to make yourself aware of and to attend literary events in your community.

WRITING CONFERENCES

If the cost isn't too high, a writing conference can acquaint the beginner with the market and give the experienced writer the contacts she needs.

The Southwest Writers Workshop in Albuquerque sponsors an annual conference with a writing contest and top-name speakers. The Mendocino Writers Conference in Fort Bragg, Calif., is a reasonably priced three days in "Murder She Wrote" territory. Shop around. Study conference brochures. Attend one or two. If you choose carefully, you'll get your money's worth.

CRITICISM SERVICES

You see the ads in Writer's Digest and other publications for writers. Which should you choose?

Many criticism services will charge you a fortune for what you could learn in less expensive ways.

Most of the national writing associations offer reasonably priced critisism services, some more intense than others. The Southwest Writers Workshop offers a low-cost service for members, and Authorlink.com and other Web sites for writers carry advertising from critique services with rates of from 50 cents to $5 a page.

Focus Your Writing

Writer's Digest has published a guide to book doctors and what they charge. Send for it. Faint when you read the prices. Then, tell yourself that you can do a better job on your own writing if you're willing to take the time to learn craft. Book doctors have many clients. You have just you. Think carefully before you write out that check for $2,000 or more.

HOW-TO-WRITE BOOKS

Writers read. They must. Part of your research time as a writer should be spent studying craft books. Writer's Digest magazine has a book club, and even if you're not a book-club person, you'll find the monthly offerings and the discounted prices hard to resist.

Even the worst craft book will teach you something. No one ever knows enough. The moment we think we know it all, we're finished, dated and dead. Writing books keep us fresh.

For fiction, two good ones are Jim Frey's *How To Write A Damn Good Novel* and Evan Marshall's *The Marshall Plan*.

Jack Bickham, has at least five craft books in print. The author of 60-plus novels, Bickham offers a user-friendly approach to complicated subjects such as viewpoint, story question and scene and sequel.

Forget titles. If you see Bickham's name on a writing book, buy it and be ready to spend the night reading it. Ditto anything by Gary Provost, who's as funny and down-to-earth a teacher as he is a writer.

Other craft books I recommend to my students are: "Turning Life into Fiction," by Robin Hemley, "Fiction Writer's Workshop," by Josip Novakovich and "Shut Up! He Explained," by William Noble.

Every writer should own a copy of Strunk and White's "The Elements of Style," which continues to be the final word on crafting prose. "Errors in English, and Ways to Avoid Them," by

Harry Shaw, offers a practical approach to correct word usage, sentence structure, spelling, punctuation and grammar.

CRITIQUE GROUPS

While not every writer needs a class, a club, a conference or a criticism service, many publishing writers I know are part of a critique group. These groups cost nothing but your time.

A good critique group can give you the kinship and the feedback you need. Investigate the possibilities. Attempt to get in with published writers and editors, if possible. Try on a group the way you would try on a new pair of shoes.

EVALUATING CRITICISM

Whether you choose a writing class, club, conference, editing service or critique group, you have to learn to recognize the ring of truth. You have to put your own feelings aside and truly evaluate the criticism.

This isn't always easy. It's best to you sleep on it, then decide in the morning what that criticism really means in terms of your work and your writing goals.

As we've already discussed, talent could be your major problem, especially when you're dealing with an editor or a critique group. If you have talent, you've probably sailed through every English course you ever took with straight A's. If nothing else, you intimidated the teacher, who probably wasn't as talented as you.

Talent is not what it takes to be a writer. It's a blessing, for sure, the frosting on the proverbial cake, but you can't sail into publication as you sailed through all those English classes.

If you're going to learn and grow as a writer, it must be with someone who knows how, not someone who just talks a good game. Talented writers especially should expect some tough criticism and some immediate results when they act upon that criticism.

No one can or should change your vision. No one can write your story for you. Use their knowledge ONLY to clarify, define or communicate your vision, your story, your way. You're looking for a guide, not a ghostwriter, not even a re-writer.

The right teacher should provide you with the necessary craft for transferring your vision, however large or small, to paper. A good editor (and often a good critique group) will tell you what to take away in order to better define your vision.

Once skilled in craft, you and you alone decide what to fill in. No one, absolutely no one, should try to take credit when you finally do it, the way all writers ultimately do, all by yourself. If a teacher, editor or critique group helps you succeed, that's great, but the one and only person who makes those decisions and revisions is you.

SUMMARY

Take care when selecting a writing class. Too often the teacher doesn't know enough about how to get published, let alone how to help anyone else. Evaluate the class in question. Is it a stroke group, an academic aerobics class, a sewing circle—or might it be a synergistic class where you can get real help?

Where is the class held? Do you really want to meet in the teacher's home? Where has the teacher published? How many writers has the teacher helped publish? What is the cost of the class?

Evaluate, not just the teacher, but the students and their critiques of fellow students' work.

When selecting a writing club, again ask yourself if you would be comfortable here. Look into national associations, then ask yourself if a local club or class can give you as much for the money.

Writing conferences and criticism services are other possibilities you might want to investigate. Research them before spending your money.

Budget for buying books on writing. No writer ever knows enough.

The right critique group may do more for your writing than a class. Investigate and evaluate criticism. The right editor, teacher or critique group can help you decide what to take out in order to focus your manuscript. No one should attempt to destroy your vision or your voice.

ASSIGNMENT

1. Investigate writers' groups in your community. Use this chapter as a checklist and don't be seduced into joining unless it's a truly remarkable class. There are other ways.

2. Look into national writing clubs.

3. Investigate conferences. Plan to attend just one, and don't spend a lot of money. Attend as many sessions as possible. Buy tapes, if available. Get your money's worth.

4. Investigate critique groups in your community. Find those with people writing the kind of material you want to publish. If you can't locate a critique group that meets your needs, consider forming your own.

By now you've either accepted or rejected the idea of a writing class, club, conference, criticism service or critique group. You subscribe to at least one writers' publication. There's maybe only one other barrier between you and your dream, that silent, scary spot within you almost every writer faces. It's called fear, and while we've touched on it before, the next chapter will show you how to recognize and deal with it once and for all.

Focus Your Writing

Bonnie Hearn

CHAPTER THIRTEEN

FEAR AND VALIDATION

Fear is a writer's natural enemy. It comes from the inside, not from agents, editors, teachers or classmates. We breed fear, and we fight it every day of our writing lives.

A poet friend of mine tries to kill it with red wine and marijuana. Fear has paralyzed him to the point that even the most minor submission transforms itself into a major undertaking.

One of my best students still waits until she's in her car before she reads my comments on her manuscripts. She's trying to prolong that moment when she has to face what, to her, is a judgment of what she's worth as a person.

"Writing is a love-hate affair," she told me. "Everything I've written so far has gone through periods when I love it for a while and then hate it. I still don't know when anything is good."

That's her insurance policy, and it accompanies every piece she writes.

A little fear can be healthy. Most actors believe some fear is necessary for a good performance. A number of writers who breeze into my class with no fear are so devastated by the slightest criticism that they never return.

"If you're not a little afraid, you know you're doing it wrong," a novelist friend of mine says.

Focus Your Writing

When fear cripples instead of drives you, you're in trouble. It can keep you from sending out your work. It can even prevent you from writing.

To deal with fear, you must first recognize its existence in your life. Why aren't you writing or submitting? No, it's not that you haven't the time. No writer has time. We *make* time.

Too lazy? Perhaps, or maybe the beer bottle, the television, are friendlier than the prospects of rejection or even success?

Your life is hell right now? Countless writers have turned bad experiences into good material.

Writing's too hard and not fun for you anymore? Fear may be forcing you to try to edit while you write. You may be allowing your knowledge of craft to intimidate you and your creativity.

Try to pinpoint and focus on your fear. If you're terrified of failure, try changing the way you think about it. In her November, 1994 Writer's Digest article, Leslie Li writes that setback and fulfillment are, for her, better terms than failure and success.

"Not only is (setback) more accurate, it is also more accommodating of second chances and lessons learned," Li said. "As for success, it is as cold, brittle and impersonal word as it is exclusive a concept; fulfillment is warmer, broader and more substantial and sustaining."

Fear of success and failure are just the beginning. You might also be experiencing fear of exposure, fear of change or even fear of discovering who you really are.

When asked why he wrote, R.D. Laing said, "So more people will love me."

Those of us who write from love and a need to be loved expose the essence of what we are. No wonder we're sometimes frozen with fear.

Regardless of where and from what your own demon originates, you'll find it easier to ignore once you're validated. You need to publish and publish now.

Anne Lamott speaks for all of us when she describes in her book, "Bird by Bird," how she felt upon learning, while in the second grade, that a poem she wrote had been published.

"I understood immediately the thrill of seeing oneself in print. It provides some sort of primal verification: you are in print; therefore you exist."

Thank you, Anne. I actually get pleasure studying my tax returns, because the IRS says it all in black and white, and the IRS doesn't lie, does it? It's not what I earn that pleases me but how I earn it, *my occupation*. Writer. Editor. Honest.

One of my closest friends is a restaurant reviewer, French cooking teacher and a fine writer. I knew her before she was any of the above. The day her first restaurant review was published, she said. "I feel like such a fraud."

"I always feel like a fraud," I told her.

"You?" She looked at me, as if she couldn't comprehend my words. "But you're legitimate."

We're *all* "legitimate," but some of us are never really certain.

You are the only person who can make yourself legitimate. You do this by giving yourself permission to make many mistakes and enjoy many rewards. What you publish doesn't matter at first. Like all writers, you need to get something in print, receive compensation for it and go on.

WRITER'S BLOCK

Too much has already been written about writer's block, which can be caused by anything from fear to laziness. Once you know you're writing focused manuscripts *that can and will sell*, you'll be amazed at how rapidly that block diminishes.

If you're still having problems putting words to paper, you might consider:

Focus Your Writing

1. Going over your plan for the week. Have you honestly noted how many hours you have free for writing, and have you broken that time into four sections for production, editing, marketing and research?

2. Determining whether or not you're writing every day. Forget the excuses, and just do it, even if it's only a paragraph a day.

3. Forcing yourself to write. Be tough. Make yourself write a paragraph on anything—a character you've never met, even why you can't write.

4. Boring yourself into creativity. Vacuum the floor. Clean the toilets. The minute you start these boring tasks, your mind will wander, and you'll be full of creative ideas. Turn off the vacuum. Throw the sponge across the room. Rush to the kitchen table and write as much as you can remember on the closest piece of paper.

5. Recording your dreams. Keep a notebook by your bed. Like poetry, dreams deal with symbols. Try to capture yours and write them down as soon as you are awake enough to do so. While they may not be the subject of your next story, getting them on paper will force you to write at least a few words every day.

6. Being your own worst judge. Washington, D.C. therapist David Oldfield has developed an exercise, *You, the Judge*, that while it wasn't intended for writers, might work for you.

With your dominant hand, make a list of the names you call yourself:
You're a fraud.
You have no talent.
No one wants to hear what you have to say,

Then, switch hands. If you're right-handed, put the pen in your left hand, and let that childlike part of yourself answer the charges in his or her own uncertain handwriting. It might be something as simple as *Sometimes you have good ideas*, or, *I like what you write*.

Listen to what this side of you has to say, and you might be able to stop judging yourself.

TWELVE WAYS TO COMBAT FEAR

The following methods will help you overcome your fears, and in the process, create a manuscript you can sell to validate yourself as a writer. Some of these methods are obvious. Some are not. All have worked for me, and many have worked for my students.

1. DO remember the four parts of your job as a writer: Creating, editing, researching, marketing. Be clear about each, and don't confuse one with another.

2. DO chart for yourself the quickest path to validation or publication. So it's an article in your local newspaper. So what? It's a credit, isn't it?

3. DO try to keep 10 to 12 submissions in the mail at all times. When one comes back, send it out again. Don't place all your hopes in one novel to one publisher, one short story to one magazine or one contest entry.

4. DO write every day, even if it's only one page or one paragraph. Demystify the process. Make it a natural part of your life.

Focus Your Writing

5. DO ask for help. Don't be afraid to seek the assistance of a qualified professional. Be sure that when you seek advice, you're ready to hear it. Refuse to be married to any scene, any phrase, any word that doesn't move your piece forward.

6. DO exercise, meditate or pray. Engage in whatever helps you clear your mind and get in touch with your spiritual self. Know that what is yours will be yours and that what should happen will happen, even if it doesn't seem that way at the time.

7. DON'T beat yourself up if you don't publish the first piece you write, and don't allow anyone to make you feel guilty. Remember, there are no victims, only volunteers.

8. DON'T talk to anyone about what you're writing or what you want to write. You'll dissipate the energy before your vision is translated onto paper.

9. DON'T show anything you've written to anyone but a qualified editor or members of your critique group. Each friend and family member has a hidden agenda, to build you up or put you down. Besides, your family and friends don't know enough to help you.

10. DON'T abuse substances. Alcohol and drugs are barriers, not bridges to publication. While these substances may aid your creativity, they'll hinder your organization and your logic, and they'll prevent your facing your writing with any degree of honesty.

11. DON'T write letters to the editor or to your family. If you must, don't consider the letters as part of your daily writing.

12. DON'T write for strokes alone. Those cute little pieces your writing classmates love may not fly on paper. Dig deep

within yourself. Use all the talent you've been given, and do the best work you're capable of doing.

Remember, above all else, *Writers write. Everyone else just talks about it.*

In order to find the validation you need, you must write, rewrite and keep writing. You have to submit and continue submitting. Starting now.

As one of my students, who began writing when she was in her 60s, said, "Don't wait until you're dead to do it."

SUMMARY

Fear is part of being a writer. Don't let it control you. Pinpoint your fear. Is it fear of failure, fear of success, fear of change? Seeing your work in print will help you combat fear.

Going over your plan for the week, writing every day, boring yourself into creativity and recording your dreams are some methods of dealing with writer's block.

Don't talk to anyone about what you're writing, and don't show anything you've written to anyone but a qualified professional.

Abusing substances is no shortcut to publication. Nor is beating yourself up for failing to live up to your (or someone else's) definition of success. Only writing, rewriting and submitting will earn the validation you need as a writer.

Very soon, maybe even now, you are beginning to understand what it takes to focus and develop a story, how to create the **promise** of a lead and how to deliver the **proof.** You are considering writing a query or cover letter, and you're getting comfortable with the challenge of marketing.

Feel free to copy and use the manuscript-submission forms that follow. If you publish your writing as a result of something you learn from this book, I'd like to hear from you.

Focus Your Writing

Next to seeing my own work in print, nothing thrills me more than seeing my students publish. It makes me feel that someone is listening, that I'm not just talking to myself when I stand up in front of that class every week. It also gives me hope for all of us who write because we love it and because we believe we have something worthwhile to say.

If this book has done its job, you finally possess the tools you need to publish, not next week, not next year, but right now.

I can't think of a better payoff.

Bonnie Hearn

APPENDIX I

MUST-READ PUBLICATIONS

Next to a check from an editor, one of these little gems in your mailbox is the best way to brighten the most rejection-clouded writer's day. They aren't free, but the returns can be far greater than the investment, if you follow the advice they offer. As you write and read, you'll find your own magazines. These are my favorites.

Poets & Writers

72 Spring Street
New York, NY 10012
Published six times a year
Yearly subscription, $18

Not flashy but far from stuffy, this magazine publishes first-rate articles and interviews. Put it on the coffee table when your former English professor stops by for sherry. Better yet, use it as a guide to markets for poetry and literary fiction, including small, university and alternative presses, and extensive contest listings.

Focus Your Writing

Writer's Digest

F&W Publications
1507 Dana Avenue
Cincinnati, Ohio 45207
Yearly subscription (without writing-club rates) $27.

Ignore the come-on ads from vanity publishers and concentrate on the contents. Solid how-to articles can lead a beginner to publication. I've read WD since it was digest-size, amazed back then that magazines actually *paid* writers real money for their material. It was here that I found both the market listing for my first sale and the craft piece that showed me how to write it.

The Writer

120 Boylston
Boston, MA 02116
Yearly subscription: $27 per year

The Writer is similar to Writer's Digest in terms of market listings and articles but not as contemporary. If Writer's Digest is your sugar daddy, this is your maiden English teacher. Just when I think I've outgrown it, I find another article that changes my mind. Maybe that's why it's survived since 1887.

The Southwest Sage

Southwest Writers Workshop
1336 Wyoming Blvd., N.E., Suite C
Albuquerque, NM 87112-5000
Subscription free with membership

If you live in the southwest, it's probably worth the $35. I list it here because the many other advantages of SWW membership are worth $35 and then some.

ByLine

P.O. Box 130596
Edmond, OK 73013
Yearly subscription: $20

Published since 1981, this supportive magazine agrees with Erskine Caldwell's statement, "Publication of early work is what a writer needs most of all in life." In line with this philosophy, ByLine sponsors numerous contests on everything from children's articles, to cowboy poems, inspirational articles, short humor, even greeting card verse. Prizes are small, but this is a great place for the beginner to start. Predominantly by and about women, articles are basic, concise and helpful.

Focus Your Writing

Bonnie Hearn

APPENDIX II

CONTEST JUDGE'S CHEAT SHEET

One advantage of judging national writing competitions is the opportunity to use (and photocopy) the forms for rating manuscripts. I've combined several of the best and come up with two cheat sheets you can use. They're great learning tools.

Before you submit your entry, judge it yourself, based on the following criteria.

ARTICLE, ESSAY

Mechanics – Have you used correct syntax, punctuation, spelling, manuscript format?

Title – Does it reflect the theme?

Idea – Is it fresh, original?

Lead – Does it hook the reader, establish the slant?

Transitions – Does the piece flow smoothly?

Focus Your Writing

Narrative – Does the piece move forward without losing the reader?

Emotional appeal – Do you make the reader care?

Writing style – Is it interesting? Does it work?

Conclusion – Is it satisfying?

Marketability – Will it sell?

FICTION

Mechanics – Have you used correct syntax, punctuation, spelling, manuscript format?

Title – Is it captivating? Is it tied to the story?

Lead – Is there a hook that captures reader interest and establishes the pace?

Point of view – Is it consistent? Controlled? Do you avoid bouncing back and forth from one character's thoughts to another's.

Main character – Is s/he rounded, well-drawn, someone who changes and grows?

Description – Can the reader not just see the setting, but experience it with every sense? Have you created fresh images?

Narrative – Do you **show**, through scenes, and not just **tell** the story? Have you paced the story through proper use of scenes and sequels?

Dialogue – Is it convincing? Does it reveal characters and move the plot? Is it balanced with narrative?

Plot – Is it original, fresh, believable? Is the resolution satisfying?

Bonnie Hearn

Marketability – Will it sell?

Focus Your Writing

APPENDIX III

MANUSCRIPT SUBMISSIONS

Focus Your Writing

Manuscript Submissions Month _____ Year _____

Title	Publication	Editor	Date mailed	Postage	Response	Date

Manuscript Submissions   Month _____   Year _____

Title	Publication	Editor	Date mailed	Postage	Response	Date

Focus Your Writing

ABOUT THE AUTHOR

A free-lance writer for over 25 years, Bonnie Hearn Hill has worked as special sections editor for The Fresno Bee, Central California's leading newspaper, since 1982. Her work has appeared in numerous publications such as Writer's Digest, Family Circle and Pig Iron. A national conference speaker and contest judge, she has taught an adult-school writing class since 1990, and many of her students have gone on to publish their own work. She is the author of The Freelancer's Rulebook, The (Expanded) Freelancer's Rulebook, Remembering Muscle Beach and a novel, Huelga House.